Understanding
Children's
Behaviour

Dr Dinah Jayson

D1102495

Published by Family Doctor Publications Limited
in association with the British Medical Association

© Family Doctor Publications 2004–2008
Updated 2005, 2008

Family Doctor Publications, PO Box 4664, Poole, Dorset BH15 1NN

Acknowledgements: Many thanks to Dr Anula Nikapota and Dr Amanda Kirby for reading and commenting on the draft, to friends who have commented on it, and to Paula Lavis from Young Minds for helping with the Useful information.

Dedication: To Esther and Daniel, Judi and Malc, Gordon, Jessica, Joseph and Jonathan

ISBN-13: 978 1 903474 20 4
ISBN-10: 1 903474 20 5

Contents

About the author

Dr Dinah Jayson is a Consultant Child and Adolescent Psychiatrist and a mother of three. As a member of the Child and Family Public Education Board (CAFPEB), she is committed to improving the understanding of mental health issues that affect children and their families.

Introduction

This book is intended for anyone bringing up, caring for or working with children – parents, carers, teachers or youth workers alike – but is addressed mainly to parents, with extra sections at the end on surviving parenthood.

Its main aim is to help you enjoy your child and your role as a parent. It aims to help you understand your child's behaviour throughout the normal stages of development up to and through primary school, and to help you deal with problem behaviours. If you understand your child's behaviour, you will be in a better position to deal with difficult situations effectively.

If you find your child difficult to manage, if parenting doesn't come naturally to you or if you just want to improve your relationship with your child, there are many strategies that can help. This book offers some solutions that you can try for yourself. It will also help you decide whether you need expert help and, if so, where to find it.

It is important to remember, however, that there is no 'right way' to sort out children's behavioural problems. No one knows your child and family set-up better than you, and not all of the ideas in this book will be appropriate, practical or relevant to your particular situation. A better understanding of your child's problems may, however, lead you to new and better ideas and solutions of your own.

The section on surviving parenthood describes how stressful parenting can be, and the effect of the parent's mood on the child. It then discusses adult relationship problems and depression, with advice about how to deal with both these difficulties.

If, having read this book, you are still concerned about your child's behaviour, or if the problem seems too much for you to handle on your own, there are various sources of advice and help which are listed in 'Useful information' on page 165.

When discussing a child 'he' or 'she' has been used randomly.

KEY POINTS

■ Understanding your child's behaviour will put you in a better position to deal with the situation

■ If you find your child difficult to manage, there are many strategies that you can try that may help you

■ There is no single 'right way' to deal with behaviour problems; every situation is unique and needs interpreting

■ There are numerous sources of help and advice to draw on

Normal development and behaviour

Normal problems

It is helpful to have an idea of how your child's behaviour may change as he develops, so that you can recognise what is normal and when you should be concerned. Many types of normal behaviour can be problematic, and your tolerance levels for these may vary more with your mood than with the child's behaviour itself. A good understanding of normal difficult behaviour can help you respond appropriately and more sensitively to your child at a time when he needs you most.

Children are not all the same

All children vary and develop in their own way. Your child may be different from his peers, but whether he is considered normal will depend on the expectations of those around him. A typical 'bookworm' may be bullied in a non-academic environment or highly valued in an intellectual one. A child who is more interested in football than work may be seen as a hero in a local community, even if he can't sit still in class,

and yet would be deemed a failure in a strict academic school or family.

A change of environment may be the solution if your child is not tolerated for being different. It is up to you to encourage your child to take pride in what he is capable of and to praise him consistently for any achievements, whether they happen to be in football or maths.

Variation between cultures

What is considered to be 'normal' will vary not only from one child to another, but also from one family or culture to another. If your child is from a different culture or background from her peers, she may be less tolerated simply because of that difference. In some cultures and families, behaviour that is accepted as normal in a boy would not be acceptable in a girl.

Boys may be encouraged to be 'macho', aggressive and dominant, whereas girls may be expected to be submissive, caring and obedient.

Increasingly, today, families are more mobile and more multi-ethnic. They are less likely to have a support network, and more likely to be exposed to cultural differences. In this context, especially if you have moved to a new area, your child may be different from her peers and be teased as a result. She will almost certainly want to be like all the others and may put herself down for being different. It is up to you to encourage her to be proud of how and whom she is.

Normal developmental milestones

It is helpful to keep a watch over your child's developmental milestones (for example, learning to walk) so that you can catch any problems early on. If you are worried about her development, consult a health professional and/or her teacher for advice. Children with developmental problems often have more behavioural problems.

What to look for in normal social developments

The following are all absolute reasons for referral to the health visitor, nurse or GP:

- At any age – any loss of skills or language
- By 12 months – no babble or gesture (for example, pointing)
- By 18 months – no single words
- By 24 months – no two-word spontaneous (non-copied) words

Relative indications (reasons) for referral to a health professional

By age two to three and onwards:

- Communication problems – language or non-verbal (for example, little or no smiling or social response)
- Poor social skills, for example, lack of or no sharing of enjoyment
- Poor imaginative play
- Lack of interest in others, 'in a world of his own'
- Lack of or poor eye contact
- Extreme emotional reactions and aggression to others
- Rigidity and difficulty coping with change, leading to distress
- Over- or under-sensitivitiy to stimuli, for example, light, sound, touch, taste
- Odd or unusual behaviours, for example, hand flapping

This book does not cover sexual development as sexual problems are not common in this age group. It is, however, discussed briefly under 'Common behavioural problems' on page 42.

Typical behavioural patterns and problems
Babies (the first year)

Initially, babies are totally dependent on you and rely on you to meet their every need. Your baby will be happiest if you respond sensitively and can calm him when he is upset. This includes making sure that he is comfortable, not only physically (warm, clean, fed and winded) but also emotionally. Babies need comfort, reassurance and emotional stability, especially when things don't feel right. You can provide this by cuddling your baby, speaking to him in a gentle voice or singing to him and distracting him from upsets by walking him around and showing him interesting surroundings. Babies need the right level of stimulation: not too much excitement, yet enough stimulation to enable them to learn, and you can work this out by observing, listening and taking your cues from your child.

There is increasing evidence from early infant studies that the patterns of interaction between carer and child can predict behaviour at an older age. Parents who overwhelm their babies with demands to 'perform' in a certain way, talk at them or do things to them in an intrusive way without watching their cues are more likely to have children who avoid instructions from parents in later life, developing attention and behavioural problems. Those who respond sensitively, watching their child and developing a gentle 'to and fro' dialogue at the child's pace, are more likely to be setting the foundations for positive social behaviour in a child. Tuning in early on to your child's needs will set him up for life. You can make a huge difference by providing this for your baby.

Attachment

Over time, babies form a deep attachment to their main caregivers, but also benefit greatly from having good relationships with other people, such as their grandparents, close family, friends and other consistent, sensitive carers to whom they can also become strongly attached.

The quality of the caring is more important than whether the person is a relative. As long as a baby's main attachment figure returns and she can develop trust that this will happen, she will thrive. If, however, your baby finds that most of the time you reject her when she needs you most, that you are unable to soothe her or that you are too exhausted to enjoy her, she will develop an insecure attachment to you. She may show this by being overly anxious and clingy (wanting to be near you all the time), being upset rather than pleased when she sees you after a separation, or even avoiding you and appearing to be independent without needing you.

If you are not the main carer, it may be difficult for you if your child seems to prefer a childminder or grand-parent to you. However, if you have to work, as long as your child gets good day care and you spend some quality time with her every day, your child will also become attached to you, and will benefit in the longer term from the role model that you provide as a working parent.

Separation

At first, babies don't understand that people still exist when they aren't there. Once your baby recognises that he is a separate person from you, and understands that you can remove yourself from him, he will also learn that you are not always there for him when he wants you. He is likely to become upset when he realises that you are not coming back and thinks that you have abandoned him. It is normal for your baby to want you to be nearby and to cry if you leave him but, with consistent sensitive caring, he will outgrow this in time. Babies need a few stable carers and have to learn that they will not be abandoned.

By six or seven months of age, your baby may begin to be wary of strangers and continue to react in this way until he's about 16 months. He'll go on wanting to be near you for years to come, but the need will be less intense by the time he is three to four years old.

Crying

At first, a baby's only way of communicating any distress is to cry, and all babies do it. Nevertheless, crying can be a distressing and unpleasant noise, and a stressed parent may feel overwhelmed by it, with feelings of anger, resentment and misery. Babies can't be 'spoiled' and are too young to be manipulative. If their needs are met, they usually stop crying. If they don't stop, this is because something feels wrong to them. Your task as the carer is to work out what is wrong and make it better, but also to recognise when you don't know what is wrong

and can't make it better. At this point, you may need someone else's help.

When your baby is crying, all you can do is go through a list of possible causes and solutions systematically, watching her responses. By watching and listening carefully, you will learn to tell one cry from another – for example, you'll begin to recognise a tired cry from a cry of pain. Crying from colic usually starts at around two to three weeks and can be particularly distressing for both of you. Your baby may cry inconsolably and won't go to sleep in the evening and may pull her knees up to her chest. Between attacks, she should seem happy and well. Gripe water may help, as will soothing and comforting your baby. However, in some cases a baby seems inconsolable. The good news is that babies usually outgrow colic by the time they are three to four months old. Your challenge is to survive that long!

Common reasons for a baby to cry

- Hunger
- Tiredness
- Wind
- Colic
- Teething
- Infections, such as coughs, colds or earache
- Cows' milk allergy

It is not always possible to find a way to stop a baby crying and you mustn't blame yourself or think that you have failed as a parent if your baby cries a lot.

Babies, like adults, are individuals and temperament is very important. Some babies have a regular sleep and feeding pattern, adapt easily to new situations and seem content most of the time, whereas others are much more unsettled and get upset by minor changes in their routine.

Some babies are naturally more difficult whatever you do, whereas others may be unwell, and it often takes a rota of unruffled adults to cope with the demands of such a child. If your baby will not stop crying, get help and advice without waiting until you are at the end of your tether.

Some parents feel so stressed that they fear that they will harm their baby, and some do. Get help when you need it well before this stage from family, friends, your community network, Social Services or other agencies. Needing and asking for help are the best way to manage the pressures and feel confident as a parent.

Toddler and pre-school (1–5)

Pre-school children can be delightful but they can also
be extremely demanding and hard work. Toddlers don't
like being apart from their carers, want attention, are
egocentric, active, impulsive and messy, constantly
interrupt and show little respect, are stubborn and
change their minds frequently, are sensitive to upset,
excitement and tension, ask endless questions and may
demoralise their parents but behave like angels for
other people.

It is important to remember that this is also an
exciting phase, as children develop physically, learn to
think more logically and become more confident
socially. They increasingly explore their surroundings,
and learn through observation and interactions with
their environment, social interactions and play. For this

to happen, children of this age need plenty of stimulation, such as:

- Books and toys appropriate for their age; these needn't be expensive – pots, pans and spoons can be much more exciting to a two year old than a 'designer' toy.

- A wide range of social contact with people of all ages, with the space, support and encouragement to develop mutually rewarding relationships.

- Exposure to new and interesting opportunities and experiences at a pace that they can cope with: contact with animals, music, water, nature, painting, parties, etc.

Your two year old – what to expect

- All 2 year olds are active and hardly ever still (this reduces to 40 per cent by the age of 4 years)
- 95 per cent want constant attention
- 80 per cent whine and nag
- 70 to 90 per cent fight or quarrel and are disobedient
- 70 to 80 per cent have temper tantrums
- 70 per cent talk back cheekily
- 70 per cent soil and wet their pants during the day
- 60 to 80 per cent cry easily
- 50 to 70 per cent resist going to bed at night
- Half wake in the night
- Half are fussy about food
- 40 to 60 per cent are jealous of or hurt a younger sibling
- 40 per cent resist sitting on the toilet/potty

Play, reality and fantasy

Children learn through play – it is the medium through which they develop socially, physically and academically. By the age of three years, they should have a fully developed sense of 'make-believe'.

This is how they learn to exercise their imagination and creativity as well as to understand day-to-day and potentially traumatic experiences, such as going to the doctors or moving house. Pretend play lets them be the 'boss' and regain control in a world where they usually have relatively little control, helping them cope with stressful situations.

Parents who try to play with their children often unwittingly take over and set all the rules, sometimes insisting that the game be played according to 'reality' principles. However, such principles may be unrealistic for a young child, and most children quickly get demoralised and give up in this situation. If you can support your child's play through observation, attention and praise, without taking over, giving advice or competing, she will take great pride in showing you how clever she is. This will not only encourage her to learn but will build her self-esteem and enhance her relationship with you. If, in play, you can help your child have more control over her fantasy world, she will be more cooperative and compliant with you in the real world.

The ability to distinguish between reality and fantasy develops with age. Young children may have difficulty remembering which parts really happened and which

were part of the game. Similarly, many three to five year olds may have an imaginary friend. This is normal and will pass with time.

When your child is playing, you don't have to be involved closely all the time. Although he will thrive on your undivided attention, he will also benefit from supportive comments while you work alongside him. Children want you to observe their progress and achievements. Your words can be very powerful in either direction, so it pays to stop and think about what you say and your tone of voice before you speak. Praise goes a long way in building and developing a positive relationship and a willing child.

Exploration and experimentation
Toddlers need plenty of stimulation so that they can learn and develop. Even if they have many exciting

toys, their curiosity will draw them to less safe areas, such as inside cupboards, loose wires and interesting-looking bottles. This is not naughtiness but curiosity, especially if it is not made clear to them what is allowed and what isn't. Very young children will not respond to being told not to touch. You can make things easier for yourself by 'child-proofing' certain areas, so that you can relax and let children explore in safety.

From early on, children want to become independent and do things themselves. They learn by repetitive experiments, so your two-year-old child may enjoy knocking things off his high chair repetitively and watching you pick them up each time. For him, this is a lesson in cause and effect, and helps him learn to think logically. This is not naughtiness, but normal exploration. Even so, you may understandably find this kind of thing irritating and parents vary as to how much of these activities they can tolerate.

What is child-proofing?

Making a place safe from children's curiosity, to prevent accidents and give carers peace of mind.

- Set up boundaries so the child can't get to unsafe areas
- Remove breakable and dangerous items
- Put child locks on cupboards/fridges/windows/car doors/medicine cabinets and other unsafe areas
- Fix stair gates on stairs
- Keep all unsafe items out of reach
- Cover up all electrical wires and plug sockets

Note that shops such as Mothercare sell all these items and can provide advice.

It is perfectly appropriate for you to set limits so that your child learns that this behaviour is not tolerated in certain settings. You can set aside special times and places for this game, and distract the child onto some other activity when you've had enough.

Children of all ages love the repetition of favourite games or songs, but this need to do things over and over starts to disappear once they are out of the toddler stage.

Understanding

Children need to have things explained to them at their own level of understanding. It is important to check that any task that you set for your child is manageable and appropriate to the stage of development that she is at currently and that she understands what you expect of her. Often, what appears to be disobedience is simple misunderstanding. Repeating the same command louder won't work in this situation. You need to try another approach.

Young children usually think that you mean exactly what you say. If you lose your temper and make an idle threat to send them to a children's home, for example, they will remember it and believe it, even if you have no such intention! Similarly, young children may not have a clear understanding of the difference between right and wrong so, although it is appropriate to teach them this, shouting and punishing them for bad behaviour, without clear explanation, will only bewilder and upset them.

Clinginess

Most toddlers are clingy. They are not being this way to irritate you, but are showing you how much they

love and need you. Behaving in this way actually makes good sense as toddlers need constant supervision while exploring their environment because they don't know what's safe and what isn't. You have to watch their every move constantly to prevent accidents. They should become less clingy by the time they start at a nursery, as they learn to distinguish for themselves what is and what isn't safe.

Children may become attached to cuddly toys or soft blankets, using them as comforters when the person whom they love most is not present. From the child's point of view, these objects are as individual and unique as people, so if she is having a tantrum about losing an old worn-out toy, offering to buy a new one will not be the same. If the toy can't be found, you will need to comfort your child over the loss, rather than simply telling her not to be silly.

It is normal for toddlers to be fearful of new situations but excessive clinginess may be related to you being temporarily physically or emotionally unavailable to your child, for instance, because of hospitalisation, long working hours or depression. He will worry that you may abandon him and may become more clingy as a result. If so, shouting at him for behaving this way will only make matters worse. You are more likely to get results if you work on your relationship with your child, reassure him that you love him and will not abandon him, and arrange for him to spend more time in the care of a trusted friend or relative. Giving him regular one-to-one time will help, even if brief, for example, a quick story before bedtime.

Avoiding tantrums

- Make sure that your child is well rested and not overtired, hungry or thirsty
- Try to keep to a comfortable, predictable routine, especially during stressful times
- Explain rules clearly in advance and keep them simple and consistent
- Keep your child active and interested with a variety of activities, a safe space to play, and attention and praise
- Plan ahead to avoid trouble, for example, on a long journey take plenty of food and drink, toys, little surprises and distractions
- Always keep a few 'special treats' as distractions for a rainy day or bored moment, for example, face paints, pavement chalks
- Avoid overexcitement
- Avoid large quantities of fizzy drinks, sweets, chocolate and food containing large amounts of additives
- Don't expect more than he is capable of, for example, don't expect him to share toys, and set limits
- If your child becomes irritable despite this (1) find out what is troubling him and resolve it and (2) notice and praise good behaviour in him or a sibling and distract him
- Give him a healthy balanced diet with plenty of fish (there is evidence that fish oils are important in normal development)

Tantrums and the 'terrible twos'

Around the age of two, children see the world as a place that should be designed to meet their own needs instantly. If they don't get what they want, it feels like a disaster, and they can scream, yell and cry inconsolably over what to you seems like nothing, especially when they get to the so-called 'terrible twos' stage. Some toddlers hold their breath in frustration during a temper tantrum, sometimes to the point of going blue or losing consciousness before making an immediate recovery. It is important to remember that this kind of difficult behaviour is normal in toddlers and three temper

What to do if your child has a tantrum

- Try distracting his attention, before the tantrum gets too bad
- Ignore him if possible and remove unsafe objects first if necessary
- Give all your attention, praise and/or a reward (for example, a biscuit) to a sibling for playing nicely! Hopefully the child will soon follow suit
- Give him an ultimatum: 'When you've stopped crying, then you can have the toy'
- Stay firm and don't give in for the sake of peace
- You can use very brief 'time out' without being rejecting by telling your child to go out of the room, leave the trouble or temper outside and then come back in without it. This can be rewarded when achieved
- If this happens in public, for example, a supermarket, leave the place (with your child, of course!) if you feel too exposed. You have to feel in control of the situation

tantrums a day may be 'routine', although you may need to seek help if the breathholding becomes extreme.

Sharing
Children aged one to two years still don't understand the difference between 'mine' and 'yours'. The concept of sharing is alien to them and they want to have everything to themselves. It is impossible to explain to a child of this age the merits of sharing, so don't expect it of your child but teach it over time. With distraction and praise for appropriate behaviour, your child will learn with age to wait for gradually increasing amounts of time and to take turns with other people.

Problems between brothers and sisters
Toddlers don't automatically love baby sisters or brothers all the time, but may feel under pressure to

behave as if they do. Even if they do love their brother or sister, these feelings may be mixed with fears that the new baby will replace them and that they will be abandoned. Sometimes, these fears will lead them secretly to harm the baby, which is why you should never leave a baby and a toddler in the same room unattended, and always make your toddler feel special and wanted in the presence of the baby.

Whenever you cuddle the baby in front of an older child, she may experience feelings similar to the jealousy of a betrayed lover. She may not be able to understand or express this clearly, so insisting she tells you 'why' she feels upset, what is bothering her or why she hurt the baby may just make matters worse, especially if you think that you are being particularly patient and she is just being difficult. She is likely to deny having done anything if challenged. She needs a clear message that you disapprove of this behaviour. If you are feeling too upset to control your temper, you could send her out of the room to a safe place until you have both calmed down.

Eventually, you need calmly to teach your child what is and what isn't acceptable behaviour, as well as to show her how much you love her, too. Giving her plenty of support, praise, cuddles and positive attention will reassure her that she is as special to you as ever. Losing your temper and shouting will only make matters worse.

Peer relationships

As children progress through toddlerhood, they will happily play alongside each other and enjoy the companionship of other children, as long as they are not expected to share. At this age, peers are seen as potential rivals and threats. Gradually, they will begin

Helping a toddler cope with a new baby

Before the birth
- Tell your child about the baby as soon as possible
- Involve your child in the planning
- Read your child stories about babies that explain the pros and cons

During the birth
- Make sure that your child is well cared for and nurtured with special treats

After the baby is born
- Involve your toddler as much as possible with the role of big brother or sister
- Teach your child how to be helpful
- Praise your child for all positivity towards the baby ('You are the best big sister in the world')
- Give your child plenty of one-to-one attention regularly without the baby
- Keep your child occupied and active – do things with her too
- Give your child plenty of love, cuddles and treats, reassure her that the baby will never replace her: 'You are the best Jenny in the world – the baby is special but she's not my Jenny'

to interact with each other from the age of about two or three years, but will prefer one friend to a group. Young children often find social situations with many children intimidating. As they become more socially confident, they will learn to feel safe in bigger groups, but there is no point in pushing your child into playing with anyone or joining in at a party until he feels ready. It is at these stressful times that children become more anxious. Sitting and watching with your child may feel like a waste of time to you, but for your child this is a way of preparing to join in. Some children learn this later than others. Be patient and supportive, and eventually your child will join in too.

Potty training

Young children start to learn to control their bowels and bladder after the age of two years. Some children take longer than others to become potty trained, and boys take longer than girls. If you give it time and patience with lots of praise and support, you will get there. Many bookshops sell helpful 'potty' stories with action dolls to match that can assist the process. There is no rush to start potty training, but it is best to start in time for entrance to nursery school, preferably in the summer months when children are more exposed to their 'bottoms' and what they do. You can keep a potty in the garden and encourage the child to 'poo' or 'wee' in it, with rewards or star charts to support

Helpful tips for potty training

- Make a toilet a fun place with books and toys to read on the potty, for example, you can get a potty that plays tunes when the child pees!
- Blowing balloons while sitting on the potty can teach your child how to 'push'
- Toilets can be scary places, so stay with your child until he or she feels safe, and stay near to help clean up
- Elasticated nappies that can be pushed down can be helpful for toddlers who want to become independent

this. Do not push it if your child is not ready. It will happen when the time is right. (Please also see the sections on wetting and soiling on pages 50–3). If your child is not potty trained after the age of four years, you should consult your health visitor or doctor.

Food fads and food refusal

Some children are fussy or faddy eaters, and the prospect of eating anything unusual can be very distressing for them. There is a fine line between insisting that they eat a wider variety of foods and understanding that they are anxious and upset, and letting them eat what they like – which is, of course, a much easier way out for the parents. Sometimes, if a child is particularly fussy about his food one day, it may be because of some unrelated upset that needs to be sorted out before the food issue can be resolved.

If you provide your child with tempting, healthy food options regularly, and praise and reward her for tasting them (without making an issue out of it), you are more likely to ensure that she gets a sufficiently nutritious diet than if you engage in battles over food. Battles will only make matters worse.

If your child dislikes the food that you offer and you can't afford the time or money to make anything else, she will eventually eat when she is hungry. You can stay firm and point out that this is what is on offer and it is this or nothing without getting into arguments. You can then accept whatever your child chooses to do, while pointing out that it is not OK to fill up on chocolate or crisps. When your child has eaten some of the food, perhaps then she can have some chocolate. You have to choose the important rules and stick to them.

You should seek professional advice if you are concerned or if your child's diet remains excessively restricted. Your health visitor or GP may need to check that your child is growing and developing normally and that there is no physical cause for her eating problem.

Primary school age

Once children reach primary school age, they become much more independent, less self-centred, and more interested in children of the same age and in activities outside their home. They have an endless need to learn and may ask you incessant questions. This is normal and not done to irritate you. If you are able to answer these questions sensibly and see them as a natural part of growing up, you will find them less irritating. You may even become infected by your child's enthusiasm and curiosity.

As your child gets older, he will understand more about 'cause and consequence' and the principles of right and wrong. The downside of this is that your eight year old may expect you to stick to exactly what you said in the past ('But you promised!'), as he still holds on to the concept that 'your word is your word no matter what'.

He will be very caught up in making sure that you stick rigidly to 'right and wrong' if you have made it clear that you expect him to do so; therefore if you can't keep a promise, whatever the reason, he is 'right' and you are 'wrong'. Unless you acknowledge this, he will be difficult to handle. Your 11 year old, however, will be able to think more flexibly and understand that, when you run out of money unexpectedly, you simply can't afford the bicycle that you had promised him.

> You have to choose the important rules
> and stick to them

Anxiety and upsets

Anxiety and upset can lead to difficult behaviour, including whining, nagging, clinging, shyness, or a refusal to go to parties or to school. For children who have difficulty confiding in their family about any upsets, stress can lead to physical symptoms such as various aches and pains. Many children, for example, develop 'tummy ache' when they are anxious about going to school. Most often, taking time to find out what the problem is at school, by talking to your child and his teacher, will lead to a resolution of the problem which could be anything from bullying to difficulties with school work. If school work is a problem, and a child

feels stupid or is criticised for something that he cannot understand, it is important to assess where the difficulty lies, provide adequate learning support and praise him for progress made. This will raise his self-esteem and decrease the upset.

Although upset behaviour is common and should improve if you handle it sensitively and firmly, you should also rule out persistent anxiety or depression (see 'Medical and psychiatric conditions', page 74). Consider these as possible causes if your child is persistently unhappy or anxious or is unable to function independently at school, despite your intervention. Children with these difficulties may feel bored, miserable and irritable. Severe anxiety can present with panic attacks, obsessional or impulsive behaviours, or phobias. These conditions are treatable and should not be missed, so if you are concerned take your child to the doctor.

If children are upset, it is important to try to understand their feelings, encouraging and praising them for even the smallest steps forward to build their low self-esteem, rather than criticising them for their failures. Teachers and parents who care enough to take time to understand and support the child can make all the difference.

Friends

It is usual for children to fall in and out with various friends over time; this is a necessary learning process for them in the course of their development. Some children seem to be loners and are uninterested in having friends but it is more common for a child to want friends but to have difficulty developing these relationships. The ability to keep positive relationships as a child is closely related to positive outcomes in adulthood, in terms of having good relationships at home and at work, and you should be concerned if your child is unable to make any friends at all.

You need to be supportive and understanding, but also must let your child learn to sort out her own problems when necessary. You can promote friendships by inviting other children over, rewarding your child for good behaviour and continuing to work on positive family relationships. Her relationships at home are the basis on which she will model her social behaviour elsewhere.

KEY POINTS

- All children develop differently and at their own pace; however, most children go through the same developmental milestones eventually

- At first, babies are totally dependent on others and most will at some stage go through a phase of not wanting to be apart from their carers

- Toddlers and pre-school children can be demanding as they develop independence and social confidence

- Primary school-age children become more interested in other children and the world around them

- Sensitive parenting is the key to developing close and trusting relationships at any age

- You have a huge amount of power and influence as a parent that can help create resilience in your child, whatever your current situation and whatever their age

Understanding children's difficult behaviours

Difficult behaviours as a plea for help

If your child feels stressed he will try to get the comfort that he needs by behaving in particular ways, such as acting more baby like, even though he may not be doing so consciously. This kind of 'attention-seeking behaviour' is usually aimed at you or any other carer who is the main 'comfort provider'. It is not done to wind you up.

Once you realise that 'bad' behaviour is often a plea for help, you will be more likely to respond in a constructive way. Although you need to teach your child what type of behaviour is acceptable and what isn't, punishing what is often a plea for help won't enhance your relationship with her. The more you can understand what your child is thinking and feeling, the more she is likely to feel understood and respond positively to your parenting. This will directly help her to develop into a responsive and sociable child (and adult). Appropriate attention is one of the most valuable things that you can give to your child.

What makes things go wrong?

Difficulties can arise if your family is under stress, for
example, when there are marital or financial problems
or when there is illness or a death in the family.
Changing circumstances can have a similar effect – for
example, moving house, the arrival of a new sibling or
when a child goes through a new developmental phase.
At these times, the atmosphere at home can alter.
Children may become upset and more demanding.
You may become more short-tempered and irritable,
and feel so consumed by your own worries that you
are less available to your child than usual and less able
to respond positively to her needs.

Children are very sensitive to their parents' moods,
often responding with behavioural problems that may
make the situation worse. The relationship between
you and your child becomes strained and, before you

know it, everyone is caught up in a vicious circle of unhappiness, with you and your child growing further and further apart. This unhelpful pattern causes further stress in itself, so it can persist even when the original source of stress has gone away. If you don't realise that this is happening, it is easy to get into the habit of criticism and blame, and this in itself can become a problem for the whole family.

Vicious circles
Your position
Many stressed-out parents or carers believe that their child is exceptionally difficult and is the cause of all the problems. In this situation, you may notice all the bad behaviour and respond negatively to it, which simply makes your child behave worse than ever.

Your child's position
Meanwhile, your child notices that you are less available and possibly more critical. He starts thinking that you don't love him any more. Initially, he will respond anxiously with more demanding behaviour. If you shout or make critical comments, it will confirm his belief that you don't love him and the result is likely to be even more 'bad' or attention-seeking behaviour.

Children need attention and prefer negative attention to no attention at all. If they always get instant prolonged attention whenever they play up, even if negative, but are ignored when they are good, they will continue playing up. This is the most effective way to teach a child to behave badly. If this cycle continues, children eventually become convinced that they are bad and unlovable and that they can get the attention that they need only by continuing to behave badly.

From his point of view, nothing he does is right. When he tries to be good, you don't notice and only comment on bad behaviour so he may well feel that he has nothing to lose by persisting with it.

'Difficult' children

Some children can seem to their parents to be particularly difficult and there are many reasons why this perception arises. Some children have more difficult temperaments than others. Trouble may also develop if there is a 'mismatch' between the parent and his or her child, such as differences in temperament and expectations – for example, a parent who is extremely house-proud and tidy will be irritated by a child who is disorganised and messy (most young children are!). Alternatively, parents who are very easy-going and arrange things at the last minute may find it difficult to

deal with a child who doesn't cope well with change and new situations and who needs structure, order and a regular routine. Such a child could develop behavioural problems in this situation.

Remember also that your child may be very different from you with regard to talents and interests. If your family is very sporty, for example, and your child is not, he is not a failure, but may just have different interests, such as music or reading. He needs to be encouraged in what he is good at rather than rejected for what he cannot do. Too many adults grow up with a sense of failing to meet their parents' expectations of them. Your child will be more confident if he is appreciated for who he is.

A child may also have an underlying problem that makes her seem difficult; this could be anything from a temperamental problem to a medical condition or

learning difficulty (see under 'Medical and psychiatric conditions', page 74). Current research suggests that about half of a child's behaviour is accounted for by underlying biological make-up (that is, genetic inheritance), with the rest being influenced by environmental factors (such as the relationship with parents and the home situation).

KEY POINTS

- Children need attention and often behave badly to gain comfort from their parents when they need it

- It is important that parents and carers understand that 'bad' behaviour in a child is often a plea for help

- Bad behaviour can develop into a vicious circle; if the parent responds only to bad behaviour rather than good behaviour, the child will continue to play up

- Some children are inherently more difficult than others

Common behavioural problems

Sleep problems

Some children sleep better than others. Just as in adults, there is a huge variation in the amount of sleep children need. Roughly a quarter of children have significant sleeping difficulties, and those who have learning disabilities or a condition such as attention deficit hyperactivity disorder (ADHD) are most prone to sleep problems. Poor sleeping can contribute to other behavioural difficulties, exhausting all the family and putting a strain on relationships. Many families accept sleep problems as a normal part of life without realising how much these contribute to behavioural difficulties. Fortunately, most sleep problems are relatively easy to treat.

Babies and toddlers

Your sleep is likely to be disrupted frequently in the first year of your baby's life, however well you manage the timing. It is essential that you get enough sleep yourself to make sure that you can cope. If your child will not sleep, try to get someone to take over while you catch

How much sleep does your child need?

These figures are average so there is a normal variance. Don't worry if your child's sleep habit is different from this, as long as he seems healthy and happy.

- A full-term newborn baby usually needs about 16 hours of sleep a day on average
- If your baby sleeps for more than this and is difficult to waken, you should consult your doctor for advice
- Two naps a day, each lasting for two to two-and-a-half hours, are usual at six months
- This can usually be cut down to one nap a day at about 12 months
- Naps should be spaced apart in the day to fit in with when you want him to get to sleep for the night – not too near bedtime so that he is not tired enough to get to sleep, or too early so that he is overtired later on
- 13 hours at two years
- 11 hours at five years
- 10 hours at nine years

up on naps. Some parents get caught up into a habit of going to bed with their children and singing them to sleep for hours and end up exhausted as a result with little time for themselves. Others sleep with the child through the night and this works well in some cultures. This may be appropriate for newborn babies, but eventually there will come a time when you will probably feel the need for the privacy of your own bedroom. The key to achieving this is to realise that

Strategies for getting your baby to sleep

The following strategies can make a big difference in getting your baby or toddler to sleep.

Getting your baby to sleep

- Try to keep a regular routine so that your baby learns when it is sleeping time

- Check that your baby is comfortable, clean, warm and fed. A larger feed at night may mean fewer awakenings from hunger later on. Make sure that she is well winded

- Put your baby in her cot, on her back and, if she is not tired, have a mobile above the cot or put music on for her to listen to until she gets sleepy. She needs to learn to be content on her own without you, and it is important for her to have times when she is left alone to amuse herself for

Strategies for getting your baby to sleep (contd)

short periods. When she gets bored she may cry, but, if she is tired, she will eventually fall asleep by herself

- Some very young babies feel safer if swaddled snugly in a blanket, and this can work wonders in a crying infant

- If she cries incessantly, or wakes in the night and cries, you will probably want to check that she is all right and settle her. Avoid prolonged cuddles at this time or it will just make it harder for her to be put down again. It also gives her the message that you are not sure she will be all right on her own. You may have to go in several times to settle her. If so, gradually extend the time between visits. She will eventually learn that it's easier to go to sleep than cry for long periods

Getting your toddler to sleep

- Set up a routine sleep time with a ritual leading up to it, ideally something that will tire your child out; a typical routine might be to go for a walk, feed her, give her a bath, put her to bed, read her a story and then leave the room with the lights out

- Taking your child for a stroll or a drive can work wonders if you are desperate

- Make it clear that staying in bed will be rewarded the next day. Do not give in to ploys to stay up

- For children who need less sleep, put them to bed a bit later, and let them stay up with the light on for a while to play. Tuck them in with the lights out later and even if they can't sleep they need to learn to stay in bed quietly. Listening to soft music may help

- Medication is not recommended to induce sleep in children, unless prescribed by a specialist

your child can learn to fall asleep without your involvement. You can teach her this by taking her to bed while she is awake, and gradually, if she won't settle, extending the amount of time that you leave her alone, with brief reassurances as necessary. Your child needs to learn to be separate from you and, the longer you keep her close, the harder the separation will become.

If you have particular problems with getting your child to sleep, sleep clinics run by health visitors can be very helpful; ask your GP or health visitor for more information.

Bedtime rules and routines for young children
Bedtime is a time of separation and will be affected by the quality of the relationship between you and your child. An insecure child will find it harder to settle. Your child may have missed you all day and want to prolong his time with you by asking for stories, toilet visits and glasses of water.

You will be most successful if you have clear rules about these and a set bedtime that you can stick to. Bedtime should not be so early that your child then wakes too early in the morning.

On the other hand, being overtired can make a child too distressed to settle at night. Your child may also want to stay up later if he is afraid of the dark or is jealous of the fact that the baby or an older sibling gets to stay up with you.

It is important to set rules and limits. For example, give him clear instructions: 'If you play quietly in your room, I'll come and read you a story when I've fed the baby. If you can't do this, it will be lights out and no story.' Be consistent and don't make him wait too long. Always give him a cuddle before lights out. If your child can't get to sleep or wakes up extremely early, he can learn to play quietly in his room rather than wake the entire household.

The above is written in the context of the prevailing British culture, where parents do not get a chance to catch up on sleep in the day. This may be entirely inappropriate for other cultures and traditions, so if you have a traditional midday siesta or other habit that suits you, do not feel that what you are doing is wrong.

Schoolchildren

Children often find it more difficult to get to sleep when their normal sleeping and waking hours change, such as in the school holidays, when they may stay up later and get up later.

If a child doesn't feel sleepy at bedtime and can't get to sleep at night, she will understandably resist going to bed. She will also have difficulty waking up in the morning and will be sleepy in the day, making her moody and irritable. The solution is to begin waking her up a little earlier each morning, then making bedtime correspondingly earlier, including on weekends. Regular physical exercise in the day can help make a child sleepy in the evening.

Medical reasons for poor sleep

Some children repeatedly wake in the night or wake up in the early morning, especially if they are under stress or are depressed or anxious. There are rarely underlying medical problems causing this, although some children with large tonsils or adenoids can suffer from intermittent blockage of their airways at night, which can lead to frequent waking and poor-quality sleep. This can cause physical and psychological

Good sleep hygiene

This refers to ways in which a good sleep pattern can be promoted. Observing these principles may be enough to resolve a sleep problem. Each point will not apply equally to everyone.

The routine

- Your child's evening and bedtime routine should work towards relaxation and sleep

- His routine on weekends and holidays should be kept similar to that on weekdays within reason

- Make sure daytime naps in younger children are well spaced and not too long (so that your child is not expected to sleep more than he needs to in total)

The physical environment

- Bedtime should be associated with warmth and cuddles, not punishment and trouble. Don't send your child to bed as a punishment, although staying up a bit later can be used as a reward

- The bedroom should be quiet, dark and comfortable, familiar and relaxing. The bed should be associated with sleep rather than play

- To help your child relax in the evening, avoid rough and tumble and excitement in the hour before bedtime

Good sleep hygiene (contd)

- Your child should be put to bed when he is tired, even if that is before normal bedtime. Don't wait until he is overtired

- Children should be able to fall asleep alone, without you being present. Some children find it helpful to listen to music or taped stories

Food, drink and setting limits to anxiety

- Don't give your child food and drink in the night. Children have to learn to eat at mealtimes, before bedtime and on waking the next day

- Avoid heavy meals or too many drinks before bedtime. Children shouldn't go to bed hungry either

- Don't give in to requests for 'just one more drink, cuddle, story, etc.' to avoid confrontation. This will just make the problem worse. Set your limits in advance and stick with them. Make sure these are followed consistently by all the adults involved in the bedtime ritual

- Avoid drinks containing stimulants such as caffeine (for example, coffee, tea, cola and cocoa) before bedtime, and limit them during the day

(Adapted from review article on sleep disorders by G. Stores (1996) *Journal of Child Psychology and Psychiatry*, Volume 37, pages 907–925.)

complications, such as snoring or other choking or gasping sounds at night, restless sleep, unusual sleep positions and daytime sleepiness with reduced performance. If you are concerned that this might be a problem for your child, get in touch with your doctor.

Night-time disturbed behaviours

These include nightmares, which may be a temporary reaction to stress (for example, after watching a horror film) or to a more serious trauma. Night terrors are different from nightmares, and in young children are alarming to watch, but clear up by themselves and are not a cause for concern. What usually happens is that the child seems to be awake and terrified of her surroundings, in which she sees frightening creatures (bees, animals, monsters, etc.). She may shout, cry and swat them away with her hands. The next day, she has no memory of this. There is no point waking your child up and explaining things, because she will sleep it off and won't remember it. Just stay with her and keep her safe and cuddled until she settles. If the problem persists, you can try to wake her up just before the usual onset of the episodes, to prevent them.

Other problems include sleep-walking which can be dealt with by making the house safe, for example, stair gates, and taking the child back to bed.

Bedwetting (enuresis)

Most children stop wetting their beds by five to seven years, but some can continue into their teens. One in six primary school children wets the bed at night sometimes (called nocturnal enuresis) and, of these, one in three wets in the daytime as well. You should be concerned if your child is still wetting after the age of six in a girl and seven in a boy, because boys mature a bit later, or if your child starts wetting after having learned to be dry.

Bedwetting has a number of causes. In some children, where there is usually a family history of enuresis, it is the result of late maturing of bladder control, and may persist into the teens. Other physical causes, including urinary infections (present in about half of day-time wetting), need to be ruled out and treated if necessary.

Children are more likely to wet if they are extremely tired or if they drink too much fluid the evening before and don't pass urine before going to bed. In most cases, wetting is stress related, especially if it occurs in a child who was previously dry. For instance, it can occur after bereavement or a change in school or family circumstances (for example, after the birth of a sibling). Daytime wetting occurs more often in girls, and may be related to anxiety getting to the toilet in school, forgetting to go until it is too late, or when laughing or giggling.

Wetting is not naughty behaviour and you shouldn't blame your child, because he can't control himself, and being told off just makes it worse. There are several things that you can do:

- Make sure that your child goes to the toilet regularly, especially before going to bed, and don't give him drinks for an hour before bedtime. A timer or regular reminders in the day can help. You may need to take your child to the toilet yourself at first.

- Sort out any difficulties or embarrassment with school toilets if your child is worried about this.

- Make a star chart or give praise and rewards for regularly going to the toilet or having dry pants or a dry bed.

- Attend to any stresses or worries that your child has. If any underlying emotional problems can't be resolved, your health visitor or GP may need to refer you for specialist child and family services. This kind of approach is usually successful, so don't despair.

- See your GP to rule out infections and physical problems.

- Ask your GP or health visitor about using a bedwetting alarm at night. This rings as soon as a child starts to wet, and so trains him to wake in the night just before he wets. Some services run specialist enuresis clinics where this can be provided.

- Speak to your GP about trying medication for short periods if your child wants to sleep over at a friend's home or go away on holiday without embarrassment. Medication works by suppressing the urge to urinate. It is not advised to take this over long periods because it may interfere with the development of bladder control.

- Make life easier for yourself by using waterproof sheets, quick drying bedlinen, etc.

Soiling (encopresis)

Soiling or encopresis is an inability to use the toilet reliably to pass bowel motions and is not normal in a child aged over four years. Faeces may be deposited in underwear, hidden in corners or smeared on walls. It affects one in 100 children and is much more common in boys.

There are many causes. Some children have never learned a normal bowel habit, perhaps because of developmental delay (learning disability) or, in some cases, because they suffer from parental neglect or abuse and have never been taught about this.

Some children have severe constipation, which leads to hard stools that are painful to pass. As a result, the child avoids the toilet because he is afraid that it will hurt, so the stools accumulate, making a bigger blockage. Liquid stools leak past, leading to incontinence and staining of underwear. It is unusual for there to be an underlying medical cause, but this possibility may need to be investigated by your doctor.

A child may have trouble passing bowel motions if she is emotionally upset. You should consider this as a possible explanation if your child was previously continent and is not constipated, especially if the behaviour is associated with smearing of faeces.

If your child has soiling behaviour, you should not criticise him, however upset you may be. He is not to blame. If he is constipated, eating plenty of fruit and fibre, having plenty of drinks and making regular visits to the toilet with praise and rewards for successful visits should make a difference. Your GP may need to prescribe a stool softener or, if the constipation is severe, suppositories or hospital treatment may be needed.

Star charts can be very helpful for younger children. For children with a fear of pain and toilets, reading them a story on the toilet may help, as will getting them to blow balloons while sitting on the toilet – this helps them push and relax.

If your child is stressed or upset, the underlying difficulty needs to be identified and dealt with. Children with developmental delay will respond to similar tactics, but these take longer to have a beneficial effect and professional help may be needed.

Your GP or health visitor may be able to refer you to a specialist encopresis clinic if there is one in your area.

School-related problems
Bullying

If you discover that your child is being bullied at school, you might wish to intervene at the school. As a parent, part of your role is to protect your child, not only from bullies in the playground, but also from unrealistic demands by teachers or anyone else. Your child one day will outgrow the need for your protection, provided that you are not overprotective and support him in finding his own solutions when he feels ready. As he matures, he may want you simply to listen and hear how he wants to deal with a situation before he tries it out himself. At a later stage, he may progress to dealing with such problems on his own without having to tell you beforehand.

Some parents may respond to bullying with anger and outrage, rushing into the school, shouting at

people and embarrassing their child. Others assume that facing bullying is a normal part of growing up, so don't intervene even when their child is clearly overwhelmed. Some parents never get to hear about the bullying because their child doesn't confide in them, perhaps thinking he'll be told he's silly for complaining. The more aware you are of your child's situation and needs and your reaction to it, the better. Most schools have an anti-bullying policy that you or your child can access, and will inform you of possible ways forward.

If your child is the bully, don't attack him. Find a quiet moment to talk through what happened from his point of view, and identify what led him to do it. He will need your support to deal with the problems that led him to turn to this, as well as a firm explanation that this behaviour is unacceptable and not to be repeated. You will need to support him in apologising and rectifying the situation from the victim's point of view, with a clear plan to prevent recurrence.

Behavioural problems at school

Behavioural problems are less common in primary school children, but need to be dealt with early to avoid labelling for the whole of the child's school career. Many children with academic or social difficulties in the classroom play the clown in class or act up, rather than admitting that they have problems and seeking help. If your child has a problem and is not assertive enough to ask for help, or unaware of his problem, even the best teachers are likely to give more attention to bad rather than good behaviour. This is because the bad behaviour is disruptive to the class. There is a strong association between learning

difficulties and behavioural problems partly for this reason. Other difficulties, such as problems making friends, dealing with bullies or adjusting to upsetting changes such as bereavement, can also lead to behavioural problems at school. As a result, a teacher may see your child as a 'bad influence' or a 'troublemaker' or believe you to be an inadequate parent. You may feel that the teacher is at fault for not recognising your child's difficulties. Sometimes, when parents or teachers are blamed, they become defensive and unable to acknowledge that they may be contributing to a problem. Another common scenario is for both parents and teachers to blame and punish a badly behaved child rather than trying to solve the underlying problem. It is important to work together with the school and share problems in a non-blaming way.

Keeping a behaviour diary

Points to include:
- What happened?
- Where did it happen?
- When did it happen?
- What circumstances led up to the event?
- Who was there?

How do I know if the problems are to do with the school, the child or home?

An important clue to establishing the nature of a behavioural problem is whether he is behaving badly at home, at school or both. Usually, it will be both, which makes it difficult to tell whether school pressures are contributing and if so how much. You may find it helpful to keep a diary noting when the behaviour problems arise and looking for specific triggers. It is important to establish whether there is a connection between academic pressures or other demands in school and behavioural problems. You may be able to work this out by asking your child and teachers about when the trouble started in relation to school pressures, and which pressures your child finds the most difficult. If your child has problems at home and at school, the best chance for a good outcome is for changes to be made in both places.

What are the causes?

Causes of behavioural problems in school include:

- bullying or abuse of any kind including sexual (in or out of school)

- unrealistic expectations (from parents or teachers, leading to rebellion)
- negative peer/family/cultural influences (for example, a prevailing view among schoolmates that to work hard is 'uncool')
- poor relationship with a teacher; boredom
- medical disorder, learning difficulty or other underlying condition such as ADHD (see later).

If the cause of and solution to the problem cannot be found, it is vital that the child is assessed by the relevant professional, otherwise an undiagnosed problem will be put down to 'naughty behaviour', and this can lead to further behavioural problems and educational failure. Teachers, school nurses, educational welfare officers and educational psychologists can be helpful with school-related problems, and health visitors, family centres and GPs can help with home-related problems. As school often can support only those with the worst learning problems, you may wish to get an independent assessment to detect specific learning difficulties (see later).

School avoidance (school refusal, school phobia and truancy)
Being out of school for a long time is a serious problem for any child and for her family. Not only is academic achievement held back, but social development may be severely affected and this may have long-term consequences as the child grows into an adult. A child who can't cope in a school setting will have fewer opportunities in life, lower confidence and is more likely to end up unemployed. The best

solutions usually involve a partnership of home, school and occasionally other supportive agencies.

The main types of school avoidance are anxiety based as in school phobia and school refusal, or defiance based as in truancy. Truancy commonly sets in when a child moves from primary to secondary school, and is not discussed in detail here.

A child may have physical symptoms, such as headaches, tummy aches, sickness and frequent visits to the toilet, caused by anxiety. These symptoms usually appear only on weekdays and in the mornings when he is due to go to school. Family problems or upsetting events in his life may trigger these problems, especially if he is particularly sensitive. If your child complains of feeling ill on school days but not on weekends, it is worth thinking of this as a possible cause, and exploring his feelings about home and school.

Features of school refusal

- Mostly anxiety related – fear of being away from parents
- Other emotional and physical symptoms
- Family history of depression and anxiety
- Parents overprotective
- Child works hard and does well at school
- Small family, or the youngest in the family

School phobia
Like any other phobia or fear, children can become afraid of going to school. There is usually a problem such as bullying or academic difficulties. Identifying and dealing with this usually solves the problem promptly, especially if it has been identified early on.

School refusal
Unlike school phobia, school refusal often has more to do with separation anxiety than worries at school. Separation anxiety refers to a fear of being away from the parents. The separation anxiety can apply as much to the parent's fear of separation from the child as the child's separation from the parent. These fears usually feed on each other.

In school refusal, the child is more anxious about separation from her parents than phobic of the school, although often there are elements of both. A child may refuse to go to school if she is concerned about her parents – perhaps because she is aware that one or both are depressed or stressed. She may worry about leaving the parent alone in this state. Parents often think that they can hide these feelings from their children, but children often see more than they are given credit for. If this picture fits your predicament as a parent, home tuition may seem to be the most manageable way forward for your child, but in providing this you are reinforcing her belief that she cannot cope at school without you and that being away from home isn't safe. It also makes it difficult for her to become independent later on in life.

The best treatment is a rapid return to school with support for the child and parents. The sooner she returns to school the better, proving to you all that you can cope apart. She will need a lot of positive encouragement and support, perhaps being taken to school daily at first by a calm adult. Being told off for pretending to be ill, or being shouted at for not going to school, will only increase her anxiety.

If your stress levels are adding to the problem, you may benefit from getting independent help for yourself (see 'Where do I go for help?', page 153).

Educational welfare officers and special needs coordinators at school are often best placed to advise and support you.

Truancy

Truancy is more of a social, educational and legal problem than a medical one and is usually part of a wider behavioural problem. Anxiety is not the central feature as in refusal and phobia. It is best dealt with by setting firm limits and managing the wider behavioural problem.

Other behavioural problems
Naughty/bad behaviours
Stealing

Even when children sense that they are doing wrong, they sometimes find it difficult to resist the temptation to take what they want. This may be a one-off incident, where they truly thought that people wouldn't mind or notice and that their need was greater. Often, however, the child feels deprived of love or material possessions compared with her peers or siblings, and will at the time of stealing convince herself that she deserves what she took and needed it, perhaps to make up for some other injustice.

It is common for children who are put under too much pressure to steal. This may be the only way they know to make themselves feel better, particularly if they feel the adults around them don't understand and

value them. If they get shouted at by these same adults for stealing, this then confirms their beliefs about being unloved and misunderstood, possibly leading to more stealing. If you approach your child's stealing as a plea for love and attention and put your temper aside, you are more likely to find a solution, although it is also important to continue setting firm and clear limits and helping her learn to distinguish right from wrong. This is especially true of children who have been in care.

Aggression

When children feel under threat, they may respond by becoming aggressive. Hitting, biting or pinching a rival may feel like the only available option. Children with learning difficulties are often more aggressive; because demands are made on them that they can't meet, they often don't understand what is wanted of them, and they do not have the verbal or social skills to respond in any other way.

Children brought up in an environment where there is violence and hostility will feel less secure and more under threat and will learn to defend themselves, like the adults from whom they learn, with shouting and violence. Aggressive reactions are often most apparent in pre-school children, but may also appear or reappear as children get older, particularly if they are under stress.

If your child tends to be aggressive, try to avoid exposing him to situations in which he is likely to feel threatened. Take time to develop your relationship, teaching him how to resolve difficulties with alternatives, such as teaching him turn-taking and to recognise when he is getting wound up, to stop and think before acting, to count to ten or walk away from trouble, and how to be assertive without being aggressive.

If, despite all this, your child continues to behave in a disruptive way, it is possible that a physical condition (such as attention deficit hyperactivity disorder, see page 85) may be contributing, and it may be worth asking your GP to refer you for a specialist opinion.

Oppositional defiant disorder

All children have moments when their behaviour leaves much to be desired, including stubbornness and tantrums. However, when this is severe or persists over several months, a child may be said to have an 'oppositional defiant disorder'. This can occur in toddlers and older children. If the problem is associated with persistent antisocial, aggressive and disruptive behaviour, hitting, kicking, swearing, throwing things out of spite, lying, stealing, cheating or hurting others with no sign of remorse, the more serious condition of 'conduct disorder' is diagnosed. Children with this problem may also behave cruelly to animals or start fires.

Conduct disorder

Children with conduct disorder often have low self-esteem, are poorly adjusted socially, may have difficulty making friends, get into trouble at school and home, and get caught up in a vicious circle of seeking attention through negative behaviour. Around four per cent of children are affected, and the disorder is most common in inner city areas.

There is usually no single cause, but contributing factors may include a difficult temperament or an inherited predisposition to aggression, and living in a hostile environment with little praise. The child may have experienced family problems (parental stress and/or hostility, marital conflict or violence, depression or another mental illness), negative life events (deaths, divorce, exam failures, etc.), environmental problems (delinquent peer group, exposure to drugs or alcohol), sexual or physical abuse, or have learning difficulties, attention deficit hyperactivity disorder or depression.

Rarely, this can become a persistent lifelong pattern, leading to teenage delinquency and adult crime. Reassuringly, only half of teenagers with conduct disorder progress down the path of adult criminality; the other half can have normal lives.

It is never too early or too late to start improving relationships with your child (see 'Finding solutions to problem behaviour' on page 109 for how to improve the situation). Various agencies can offer support, including the Child and Adolescent Mental Health Service (CAMHS) through your GP, social services, voluntary agencies and other community groups. Family centres such as SureStart may be particularly helpful for young families.

Upset/anxious behaviours
Fearfulness and anxiety
If your child is anxious, she may insist on doing things in a certain way, and may withdraw from new and unfamiliar situations, including people. This can get in the way of making friends and having a social life. If your child is like this, it is essential for you to work on gradually exposing her to manageable social situations with support, encouragement, praise and rewards. The school may be able to work on this with you if you discuss it with your child's teacher. Sometimes a school

can arrange a 'buddy' system, whereby another pupil takes your child under his wing. The school may even organise social groups that your child can join. Ideally, these would be linked to an activity that she already enjoys. Learning a new hobby can also help to boost a child's self-esteem and reduce her anxiety.

If your child suffers from anxiety, you will need to help her fight this by setting small manageable tasks that lead her in the right direction, and giving her praise and rewards when she accomplishes them successfully. Remember that her anxiety may be caused by some event in her life or other upsets that will need to be dealt with separately.

Some children can become very obsessional and can get caught up in compulsions to wash their hands or check things repeatedly. If her anxiety prevents her from living a full life and significantly interferes with her activities, especially if the problems persist, you should seek professional help. She will need to be referred by the GP to a clinical psychologist or child mental health worker for assessment.

Some children take a natural fear of certain animals or insects to extremes, refusing to leave home for fear of encountering such creatures or being terrorised by the thought. This kind of fear or phobia may need professional therapy and you should speak to your GP about this.

Regression or not acting their age

When children are anxious or stressed, they respond in many different ways. Some children wish that they were a baby again so that they could be looked after as they were then. For example, a child may lose certain skills, wetting or soiling when he was perfectly clean and dry before. This regression is not naughtiness, and is not consciously done, but is caused by anxiety.

Similarly, some children will seemingly put on a babyish or whining voice when stressed or upset. This is not done to wind you up, and your child may be unaware that he is doing it until it is pointed out to him. This type of behaviour is most common in pre-school children, but can also occur as children get older, particularly when they are under stress. Another common behaviour that can worsen under stress in this age group is obsessional behaviours, such as walking on cracks in the pavement, or compulsive behaviours, such as touching all the railings while walking past a fence. Even adults have such behaviours when stressed! Support, encouragement and sympathy, together with help and rewards for more acceptable behaviour, will be much more effective than a telling off.

Unexplained aches and pains

Emotional distress can surface as physical aches and pains, especially in young children or those who have difficulty talking about their emotions. This may also occur with children who have friends or relatives with physical symptoms, perhaps because they are exposed more to illness and worry more about it. Most adults are familiar with the churning sensation in the stomach before exams or a similar ordeal, and this is not dissimilar from the stomachache complained about by children anxious about going to school. Children are rarely conscious of being manipulative and do not put on symptoms merely 'for show'. However, the behaviour can develop into a habit as a way of getting attention.

If you respond to the pain as if it were a symptom of a medical condition, keeping your child off school and making a fuss of her, she will find herself rewarded for giving in to anxiety. She will then be more likely to repeat the behaviour and this doesn't help her to cope with the anxiety at school. If, on the other hand, you force her to go to school without discussion, you are not addressing her anxiety sensitively and this could make matters worse.

Shouting at your child will lead her to think that she is not loved or trusted, making her emotions – and therefore pain – worse, as well as impairing your relationship.

A child who feels that she isn't believed is more likely to exaggerate her symptoms so as to ensure that she is listened to. She may be driven to lying about symptoms if she feels that it is the only way to be heard that is rewarded. If this behaviour continues it could cause problems later on – for example, if your child develops symptoms of a real physical illness and you don't believe her, she may not get the necessary treatment.

You need to work with your child in helping her fight the anxiety or upset: listen to your child's complaints about aches and pains, but move on to a discussion of underlying worries, and then help your child think through the options of how to tackle the underlying problem and find solutions. Helping your child find other ways to express her distress through words, drawings or play, while tackling the source of stress directly as well, should help to resolve her symptoms. By adopting this approach, you avoid blame, build on your relationship of trust with your child and teach her how to overcome powerful upsetting emotions. A trusted friend or relative may be able to help, but a professional outside the family may be needed if problems persist. A school nurse, health visitor, educational welfare officer or referral to a child mental health team via your GP may be needed.

Strange behaviours

Some children go to extraordinary lengths to get attention and may act in unusual ways to attract this.

Other types of strange behaviour such as inappropriate laughter, swearing, odd movements, gestures or mannerisms, unusual or avoidant eye contact, and other socially inappropriate behaviour can be involuntary, and part of an underlying disorder. In most cases, the behaviour can be explained simply by looking at the situation and the developmental level of your child. However, if your child's behaviour can't be explained, he doesn't settle or he behaves very differently from other children of his age, you should seek medical advice. He will need to be assessed to

rule out an underlying condition such as autism or a rare chromosomal abnormality (see 'Medical and psychiatric conditions', page 74).

Drugs, solvent abuse and alcohol

Drugs, solvent abuse and alcohol can also be a common cause of strange behaviour. The behaviour generally resolves when the effects of the substance wear off. Substance abuse is unusual in primary school-age children but is on the increase and linked to early smoking. It is more common in children with pre-existing upsets and behavioural problems, especially if they are part of a delinquent peer group. Look out for a change in personality, money going missing and behaviour that is out of character. There are very helpful substance misuse services that can advise.

Sexual behaviours

It is common and normal for children to become increasingly interested, first in 'bottoms, willies, poo and wee' and, as they approach secondary age, in sexuality generally. As toddlers, boys and girls may mix with each other indiscriminately, but, usually by reception age, boys and girls tend to segregate, only to become re-interested in each other again as they approach secondary school.

There is, however, nothing 'wrong' with tomboys or boys who prefer being with girls – this is part of normal variation so do not worry if your child is different. You need be concerned only if your child becomes increasingly distressed about 'being the wrong sex', and increasingly behaving like the opposite sex in extreme ways (for example, boys persistently wanting to wear dresses, or use girls' toilets at school). Gender identity disorders are extremely rare but do often need specialist support from an early age, usually accessed via a Child and Adolescent Mental Health Service (CAMHS).

Although it is common for boys in particular to 'fiddle with their willies' virtually as soon as the nappy comes off, and for children to play 'doctors and nurses', exploring their bodies out of curiosity, it is not normal for primary school children to display overt sexual behaviours such as masturbation for sexual arousal, or interacting sexually with other children. This sort of behaviour, especially if recurrent and persistent, is usually a sign of exposure to trauma, abuse or sexually explicit material. Do not automatically assume that your child has been abused, however. It is increasingly common for children to find their way to pornographic magazines, videos or 'bigboobs.com' on the internet, and adults have to be increasingly careful to protect their children from inappropriate sexual exposure.

If your child displays sexualised behaviour, do not get angry or condemn him. Explain about the inappropriateness of the behaviour and set limits on it. Enquire carefully from him and those around him what caused the behaviour. The cause can often be removed with little damage, but, if your child has been abused, especially over a long period, he may be too scared to tell you, and other behaviours demonstrating his distress will emerge, for example, low mood, social avoidance, self-harm or other behavioural problems. Sexual abuse is very damaging to a child and must be stopped immediately. Your first job is to protect him from further abuse if you suspect it. There are a number of agencies such as the NSPCC (National Society for the Prevention of Cruelty to Children) that can advise you of where to get help locally (see 'Useful information' on page 165).

The next step is to be emotionally available to listen non-judgementally and provide support. You are likely to need support for yourself to be able to manage this, especially if abuse is in the family as is often the case. The worst thing to do is pretend that nothing happened, because this cuts your child off from the support that he needs from you and leads to the worst outcomes. You can make all the difference by being present and supportive.

KEY POINTS

- Children have different behavioural problems depending on their age, and can regress under stress

- Young children are more prone to sleeping difficulties, bedwetting or soiling

- Schoolchildren may experience bullying (or bully other children themselves) or have other problems with school such as school refusal or phobia, which can present with physical symptoms and anxiety

- Other problem behaviours include stealing, aggression and truancy

- Strange behaviours may be the result of substance abuse, or part of an underlying disorder needing professional help

- Many of these behavioural problems can be avoided or dealt with easily, especially if caught early

Medical and psychiatric conditions

Children of all ages behave badly from time to time, especially when they are tired or ill. In younger children, this may simply be the result of something minor such as teething or an earache. However, a specific underlying condition may be responsible for persistent bad behaviour. Many conditions, such as depression and **a**ttention **d**eficit **h**yperactivity **d**isorder (ADHD), are much more common than previously believed, and even autism, which is rare, is much more commonly diagnosed today, because it is much better understood. Even in a mild form, it can lead to extreme behavioural problems that formerly may have been dismissed as bad behaviour.

If your child has an underlying condition affecting her behaviour, it is important to identify and treat this as early as possible, to prevent the bad behaviour from becoming established, and to give your child the best chance to get the help and resources that she needs. This way, her difficulties will not be worsened by frustration at a lack of support and understanding.

The main conditions of primary school-age children are covered in this chapter, focusing on treatable problems that benefit from early identification and intervention.

Physical problems as a cause of behavioural difficulties
Hearing loss

If your child seems to ignore you when you ask him to do something, especially from a distance, it is worth getting his hearing tested by a health visitor, school nurse or GP. In all age groups, but especially younger children, poor hearing can lead to behavioural problems. Common causes include recurrent ear infections or glue ear (in which a sticky fluid builds up in the middle ear, interfering with the flow of sound). The child can't hear what is said to him, so appears not to listen until shouted at. Most hearing problems in children are easy to treat. It is important to identify this problem early, because persistent hearing loss can affect speech development and school performance.

Poor eyesight

If your child doesn't see things that the rest of the family see or tires easily when reading, you should get his eyes tested. Sight problems in children include difficulties seeing far or close up, or seeing words swimming in the background. These can lead to eyestrain, headaches, tiring easily, work avoidance and trouble with parents and teachers, without anyone realising that the child just needs to wear glasses.

Food intolerance and allergies

Although a food allergy or intolerance may sometimes cause behavioural problems in children, this is very

Differences in food allergy, intolerance and aversion

Food aversion
No physical reaction to the food. Child dislikes and avoids the food, for example, broccoli

Food intolerance
The child has a physical reaction to the food, for example, over-stimulation. You will notice behavioural problems or headaches when the child consumes the food, for example, fizzy cola

Food allergy
The child has a physical reaction to the food. The immune system overreacts to cause itching, rash or breathing problems. Symptoms can be very severe, even life threatening, for example, nut allergy

uncommon. Certain foods do wind some children up, including stimulants such as coffee, tea and cola drinks in excess, and some food colours and preservatives (especially tartrazine, a food colouring found in some sweets and drinks) can have a similar effect. If you think that a particular food upsets your child, he can avoid that food provided that he can still eat a healthy, varied, balanced diet. You shouldn't put your child on an extremely restrictive diet (for example, cutting out all dairy products) unless it is under the supervision of a doctor or a nutritionist who specialises in allergies.

There is some evidence that fish oils may help children with behavioural problems and no evidence to suggest that this is harmful, so it may be worth trying, especially in children with neurodevelopmental disorders.

Neurodevelopmental disorders

There is a much greater understanding and recognition today of a group of developmental difficulties that often cluster together and lead to behavioural problems if not identified and treated. These include specific learning difficulties, such as dyslexia and dyspraxia and speech delay, and disorders such as ADHD (attention deficit hyperactivity disorder), autistic spectrum and other rare developmental disorders, which are all much more common in boys than in girls.

Previously, many of these children would have been labelled as lazy or naughty. Many have dropped out of school and are over-represented in the criminal system, often because they become aggressive and defensive after years of being told off without understanding why. They are also more at risk of psychiatric complications especially if untreated (for example, depression and anxiety).

Today, these conditions are easily identifiable and treatable, often leading to normal healthy lives, instead of trouble, failure and misery for individuals and their families.

These disorders can be missed in children with behavioural problems, so, if your child is odd or if behavioural problems persist despite parenting and/or school interventions, see a specialist.

Tic disorders

Tics are involuntary movements or sounds that are repeated over and over again, but can be temporarily suppressed. About 10 per cent of children have persistent tics at some stage (for example, eye blinking – often stress related) but in some they can persist and rarely (5 per 10,000) they can be part of Tourette's syndrome, a more complex disorder with verbal and movement tics, obsessive–compulsive symptoms and other neurodevelopmental problems.

The outcome is generally good (tics can improve with age) and persistent or complex tics are treatable with specialist intervention. For persistent complex tics, medication can be very helpful if other approaches such as lowering stress do not work. It is important to identify the problem rather than blame the child for involuntary tics.

Obsessive–compulsive disorder

This is another treatable neurodevelopmental disorder characterised by obsessions (for example, about cleanliness and infection) and compulsions (for example, hand washing) and may be associated with anxiety, depression and specific learning difficulties. If these symptoms persist, especially if they are distressing, referral to a paediatrician or Child and Adolescent Mental Health Service (CAMHS) specialist should be made through the GP.

Learning difficulties

Learning difficulties are not a form of mental illness nor are they a psychiatric disorder. However, the risk of mental health and behavioural difficulties is much greater. This is especially true if there is an additional complication such as autism, epilepsy, a sensory impairment (such as blindness or deafness) or a speech disorder. For this reason, children with learning difficulties have much greater needs for support than other children. When these needs are not met, or when more is expected of the child than she can possibly manage, her behaviour is likely to deteriorate.

General learning disability

In the past, general learning disability was called 'mental handicap' or 'mental retardation'. Now, other terms used include global or general developmental delay in younger children and global or general learning difficulties in school-age children. General refers to overall impairments, affecting all areas of learning, rather than to isolated specific areas.

The affected child is usually slow to develop and is less bright academically than other children, as measured by standardised developmental and intelligence tests.

The intelligence quotient or IQ is the standardised measure most used to assess intelligence. There may be a physical disability as well, as in cerebral palsy – a condition in which the child's neurological system is damaged from birth, leading to movement and intelligence problems of varying severity, for example.

The effects of the learning disability can range from mild (an IQ of 70 to 80) to severe (an IQ of 40 or less). A normal average IQ is 100 ± 10, and a gifted person may have an IQ up to 150.

Causes of learning disability include inherited disorders (such as Down's syndrome or fragile X syndrome, both chromosomal disorders), infection or injury before or during birth as in cerebral palsy, or a head injury. In half of all cases of learning disability, however, no cause is found.

Children with a general learning disability are usually diagnosed early on, before nursery school, although milder forms may not be recognised until secondary school. Your health visitor and GP should be able to recognise delayed development and refer you to the child development team, who can diagnose any underlying condition. Your child will need a special school or extra help in a mainstream school, as well as regular assessment and monitoring.

It is common for parents to feel guilt, worry, stress, depression or burnout when their child has a learning difficulty. These feelings can spread to any other children they may have, and the whole family can be affected. Often, families feel the need to pretend that everything is OK when it isn't, which in itself can put everyone under a lot of strain. It is important to find the right balance of having a positive attitude, acknowledging upset feelings and having realistic goals so that the whole family can still get on with leading as normal and enjoyable a life as possible.

Specific learning difficulties

Children with a specific learning difficulty, despite having normal intelligence, have difficulty with one or more tasks such as reading, writing or maths compared with the level predicted for that child's age, intelligence and schooling. Despite being of normal intelligence, these children often fail academically because of this specific problem.

Specific learning difficulties tend to run in families and are more common in boys than in girls. They may be subtle and often go unrecognised by the school. As a result, affected children may get labelled as lazy, immature, difficult or unmotivated and may have a blighted school career.

The children often have very low self-esteem, believing themselves to be 'stupid' or 'thick' when they are not. As they are bright, they are fully aware of what they can't do, which is very frustrating and demoralising for them, especially if they are teased by other children or told off by unsympathetic adults.

Specific learning difficulties can often lead to behavioural problems. Sometimes a child with a mild specific problem that is not recognised will be more frustrated and upset for failing to meet high expectations than a child with a general learning disability in whom it is obvious that the child has special needs, and where less is expected of him.

School support

Schools have varying attitudes to specific learning difficulties, with some providing extra help and support automatically and this helpful approach is increasing as these conditions are increasingly recognised. (Universities now increasingly admit and provide extra help for pupils with special needs.) Other schools, however, may deny that there is a problem, dismiss it as mild, suggest that the child will grow out of it, blame the parents for any bad behaviour or dismiss the parents as neurotic if they point out their child's problem. It is hoped that, with more public awareness of these conditions, this attitude will disappear in time.

If a child has a behavioural problem some teachers assume that this is causing the learning problems and not the other way around. Often, however, the relationship does go both ways. The educational failure is not the child's fault if his extra needs are not recognised or met with extra help. This can be a real problem for schools and families if there are not enough resources to help. Schools will help children with severe problems but others may not necessarily receive the help that they need.

The mismatch in expectations can lead to conflict, the school having to demonstrate that the child can access the curriculum while parents often want the school to maximise their child's potential. It is often more important that the parents and school compromise to work together productively and creatively within resources available than expose the child to anger and disagreements between themselves.

Dyslexia (specific reading delay)

If your child is bright but under-achieving, he may have dyslexia, which means he has difficulty with reading. Dyslexia is often associated with clumsiness (which overlaps with dyspraxia – see page 83), poor right–left orientation, delayed speech development in early childhood, and a family history of developmental reading, speech or language disorders. Your child may have difficulties with spelling, and may remain a poor speller into adulthood despite being very intelligent. He may have poor visual memory, poor hearing memory or both, which makes it difficult for him to learn to read and spell. A special needs teacher or psychologist can test for this.

If dyslexia is diagnosed, your child will need extra help in school. Understanding the problem, lowering expectations and pressure, and providing extra support – such as computers, special teaching and extra time in exams – can be very helpful. Recognising and tackling the child's problems will often produce obvious improvements in behaviour.

Dyscalculia
This is a specific difficulty with maths. It can be extremely specific, for example, an inability to learn multiplication tables. Similar principles apply as for dyslexia.

Dyspraxia
Also known as developmental coordination disorder or clumsiness, dyspraxia is one of the most common developmental disorders, affecting six per cent of schoolchildren, mostly of normal intelligence. The term covers coordination problems with fine motor skills, such as difficulty with shoelaces or handwriting, and/or gross movement skills, such as difficulty with team sports and being accident prone, spilling drinks.

The child often has difficulty with visuospatial understanding, including sense of direction, perspective and three-dimensional space. He may get muddled about the sequence of things, may be disorganised and may often lose things.

Some children are also unable to cope with more than one or two instructions at a time and may have a poor understanding of interpersonal space so that they get physically too close to people without realising that they are doing so. A child with dyspraxia is often slow with his work and tires easily, especially with handwriting tasks. Copying from the board is very difficult because he loses his place on the page and the board, having to start over each time he moves his eyes from the board to the paper. He easily loses heart and gives up, especially if he is told to stop being lazy, speed up and write more tidily. This can make him very anxious with low self-esteem.

Most professionals familiar with the condition have the expertise to make the diagnosis that is now more widely recognised, using clinical judgement and stand-ardised tests of motor coordination. Once diagnosed, there is a great deal that can be done to help such as:

- allowing extra time for classwork and, if possible, for exams too
- enabling the child to work on ready-copied sheets rather than copying from the board
- praising what can be done rather than criticising what can't
- allowing the use of a computer when possible and helping a child to learn to touch-type
- providing a slanted work-top – this eases pressure on the pencil – special easy-grip pencils and special scissors if necessary.

Extra help and occupational therapy can make a big difference too. A child's behavioural problems will often improve once help has been provided.

Language and communication difficulties

Language difficulties have many forms and causes. Some children find it difficult to understand speech (receptive problems); others have difficulty talking, finding words or pronouncing words. In some language disorders, children misunderstand what is being said, for example, taking everything literally, to the word – such as if he is told 'I'll only be a couple of minutes', the child will get upset if that person takes longer than exactly two minutes. If you find yourself upsetting your child regularly without understanding why, this may be what is going on.

Language and communication difficulties may be associated with other conditions, such as dyspraxia (see page 83) and autism (see page 99), and can cause behavioural problems. The behavioural and learning problems usually occur because children with language disorders may be very frustrated at their inability to communicate, especially if they are bright and this is not recognised. Identifying the problem and providing specific help and support (for example, speech and language therapy) are vital.

Attention deficit hyperactivity disorder (ADHD)

Many children behave badly or out of control when their parents do not discipline them. Most respond to discipline and clear, consistent rules (see later). Some, however, remain difficult to control even with tight discipline and excellent parenting. These children are likely to have attention deficit hyperactivity disorder (ADHD). ADHD is increasingly being recognised in this country as a cause of severe behavioural problems. Other similar terms are ADD(H) (attention deficit disorder [hyperactivity]) and hyperkinetic disorder (a more severe variant). Until recently, the condition was under-diagnosed in this country, compared with the USA where it is perhaps over-diagnosed. This is because the condition of ADD is diagnosed and treated medically in the USA even if the hyperactivity component is absent, and if the symptoms are not as pervasive across situations (see criteria below). In the UK, most children with ADD did not get treated with medication, although this is changing in the light of a trial in the USA showing the effectiveness of medication in ADD as well as ADHD.

Around one per cent of children are severely affected and around five per cent have a milder form of the condition. The condition is present from pre-school age, and is much more common in boys (five to one). It is important to recognise it, because affected children can be incorrectly labelled as 'naughty'. With the right treatment, most children with ADHD can lead a normal life.

What are the symptoms?

For a child to be diagnosed with ADHD, he or she has to have significant symptoms from toddler age, and these symptoms must be present in virtually all situations. These symptoms include the following.

Hyperactivity/overactivity

A hyperactive child can't sit still or quietly for any length of time; even if he is sitting down, he will constantly fiddle, fidget or make a noise. This will be particularly noticeable at mealtimes or in school, where other children of a similar age are able to sit quietly and eat or work. Even when playing, a child with

ADHD is constantly on the go. He may be accident prone because he is likely to be climbing, running or jumping around more than other children, but also because it can be associated with coordination difficulties. The positive side of this is the great enthusiasm, energy and tirelessness that can be a real asset.

In girls it is often much more subtle and can manifest as over-talkativeness or fiddling.

Poor concentration/distractibility
Affected children have a short attention span and can't concentrate for any length of time, although this may improve as they get older. They find schoolwork particularly difficult for this reason, and tend to underachieve, despite often being very bright. The

slightest distraction interrupts their concentration, and they may not be able to stick at any task for more than a few minutes at a time. They often forget what they were in the middle of doing, so may appear to wander aimlessly from one distraction to another. Often their school books will be noticeable in that all the work is unfinished, hurried, messy and disorganised. They appear not to listen to what they are told, which infuriates the adults around them.

Impulsivity

Affected children seem to rush headlong into things without thinking, which can sometimes involve risk and danger or saying things that they later regret. They may talk to strangers (despite knowing that it is not allowed), blurt out answers out of turn in class, run

heedlessly across a road or climb dangerous obstacles. They often know that this is wrong, but do not remember to think first at the time. They can constantly let themselves down despite their best intentions, which is frustrating for all involved.

What is the cause?

The condition is the result of a problem in the brain affecting the regulation of attention, concentration and activity levels. Its exact nature is unknown, although the parts of the brain involved seem to be the frontal lobes, which contain a chemical called dopamine. This area of the brain usually switches off distracting signals and urges. If it doesn't work properly, children can't suppress irrelevant signals and urges and therefore follow them through.

The condition tends to run in families, although often relatives have it only partially and it has an 80 per cent heritability. Social deprivation, neglect or abuse in children as well as high anxiety can look like ADHD, and it is important to distinguish this from ADHD; they can often coexist, so it is important to tease out both elements. Although some food additives such as colourings (E100–150) like tartrazine, preservatives (200–297), cola drinks and chocolate can make the symptoms of ADHD worse or cause similar symptoms in some children, there is no evidence that these are the cause of the condition.

How is it diagnosed?

There is no clear test for ADHD, although there are some questionnaires that can help screen for it. The box on page 91 summarises the criteria, but do not automatically assume that your child has ADHD if he scores positively on this. As the symptoms are normal in toddlers and can be present for other reasons, it takes an expert in child development or psychological and medical problems to make the diagnosis. Your GP should be able to refer you to a specialist clinic.

How serious is ADHD?

ADHD can have a devastating effect on a child's life if it remains untreated. The child is often in trouble and has difficulties at school, at home and with friendships, undermining his self-esteem and motivation to succeed in life. This has a negative impact on the whole family and school. It can impair driving performance later on and, in severe cases, it can lead to delinquency and drug addiction.

British diagnostic criteria for ADHD

Attention problems
Six or more of the following, for at least six months, inconsistent with age and level of development:
- Poor attention to detail/careless errors
- Often fails to concentrate
- Often appears not to listen
- Often fails to finish things
- Poor task organisation
- Often avoids tasks that require sustained mental effort
- Often loses things
- Often distracted by external stimuli
- Often forgetful

Hyperactivity problems
At least three of the following:
- Often fidgets or squirms on seat
- Leaves seat in classroom when expected to be sitting
- Excessive inappropriate running or climbing
- Often noisy/has difficulty being quiet
- Persistent overactivity not modulated by request or context

Impulsivity
At least one of the following.
- Often blurts out answers
- Fails to take turns in games or wait in queue
- Often interrupts
- Often talks excessively

If treated, however, the outcome can be excellent with up to half of the children outgrowing their symptoms eventually. In others, although ADHD never goes away entirely, the symptoms do improve with age. Adults with ADHD may have difficulty concentrating and sitting still without fiddling.

Problems such as delinquent or criminal behaviour, difficulty with relationships and substance abuse are much less likely to develop if the condition is treated at an early stage. Most people can live a relatively normal life with treatment.

What is the treatment?
After the condition has been recognised and understood at home and at school, the main treatments are as follows:

- Medication
- Behavioural treatment:
  - work with the child at home and school
  - parent training in groups or alone
  - family work
- Liaison with school
- Treating other problems and complications.

In 1999 a large multicentre study in the USA showed unequivocally that the best treatment for ADHD, especially if complicated by oppositional behaviour (see page 64), is the use of appropriate medication. Historically, in the UK, we have saved medication for the last resort, particularly as families are understandably not keen to medicate their children. This study suggests, however, that behavioural treatment alone is likely to be relatively ineffective, except in children with ADHD and anxiety symptoms who do not have oppositional behaviour, where medication can be less helpful.

With medication children are much more likely to be able to respond to behavioural interventions which can make a big difference in children with oppositional behaviour. A combination of treatments is usually best in the long term.

Liaison with the school and treatment of other problems are always crucial.

Early evidence suggests that a crucial component of positive outcome is the parent's ability to avoid blaming and criticising the child, yet to parent consistently and firmly with the support of the child's school.

Medication
Stimulants
Although medication alone may not be a solution to all the problems, stimulant medicines such as methyl-phenidate (Ritalin) can dramatically improve the symptoms in up to 90 per cent of children, and are the most effective form of treatment in most cases. Methylphenidate works by stimulating neurotransmitter receptors in the brain such as dopamine, which directly affect attention, concentration, impulsiveness and hyperactivity. This literally allows your child to stop and think, perhaps for the first time in his life. This then enables a child to settle down and live a more normal life, build educational and social skills, boost self-esteem and restore hope.

Side effects
Over five million people over 40 years have been treated with stimulant medications, with no long-lasting adverse

What strategies can parents and teachers use to modify behaviour in ADHD?

- **Parenting style**
  Be firm and consistent, but warm and praising (see 'Finding solutions to problem behaviour', page 109).

- **Avoid blame and criticism**
  You may be cross with the behaviour, but don't let this mar your relationship with the child. Help him fight the behaviour by setting firm limits and consequences rather than having an argument with him.

- **Parent support group**
  Access your local ADHD parent support group for help and advice.

- **Reduce distractions**
  Keep his environment uncluttered.

  Set him realistic tasks.

  Remind him gently but firmly of what he needs to do if he gets 'off task'.

- **Increase structure and routine**
  Children with ADHD cope better if they have a clear plan of action and frequent supervision and feedback.

  Keep firm boundaries and consistent rules.

- **Provide adult supervision**
  Children with ADHD are easily led into trouble. Keep an eye on them, and do not let them wander the streets unsupervised.

- **Keep tasks short and review frequently**
  Break up a long task into small ones, with frequent reviews to check that work is on target.

  Checklists, reminder alarms and diaries can be very helpful.

What strategies can parents and teachers use to modify behaviour in ADHD? (contd)

- ### Focus your child's attention

  #### 1. Communication

  - Make sure that your child is giving his full attention to you when you are asking him something: talk face to face and make sure that he isn't distracted. You may need to hold his head or shoulders gently to achieve this. Don't call out instructions to him if he's not in the room, as you'll probably be wasting your time. He won't register.

  - Practise communicating very simply and briefly in sound bites. 'Get the milk from the kitchen, please.' Not 'Robert, stop fiddling with the cutlery. Get the milk and set the table. Come on, get on with it, we're late for school. Hurry up. Don't forget you have PE today and your shorts are on the landing.' He is likely to have forgotten what to do next after all of this.

  - Check that he understands what you want him to do by asking him to repeat what you asked of him before you let him go.

  - Follow up and praise him immediately before asking him to do the next task. 'Well done. Now, please pour some out in these cups. Great! Now . . .' You can make it fun by trying to do it in a set time as a game if time is short.

  #### 2. Stop and think

  Teach your child to stop and think, and remind him of this regularly.

  #### 3. Self speak

  Ask your child to try 'self speak' to help keep him focused. Get him to ask himself questions and supply the answers to help him stick to the task in hand: 'Where am I? Where am I supposed to be? I'm in the TV room and am supposed to be in the kitchen. OK, I'm now in the kitchen. What am I supposed to do? Oh yes, fetch the milk from the fridge. OK, I have the milk. What am I supposed to do with it?' etc.

effects reported. Five to ten per cent of people get short-term side effects that are reversible on stopping the medication. These include slowing of growth, loss of appetite, poor weight gain, difficulty sleeping, headaches, daydreams and tics. These are usually minimal, and the medicine can always be stopped if it does not suit your child. Children must have their height and weight monitored regularly for this reason.

Addiction and licensing

The medication is not addictive in children and works best with consistent parenting. It is not licensed for use under the age of six. It is a controlled drug (prescription only), because it can be peddled illicitly for its paradoxically stimulant effect in adults, especially if modified chemically. Recent research has shown that treatment with methylphenidate can prevent addiction to illicit drugs, which can be a common complication of untreated ADHD.

Prescribing methylphenidate

Methylphenidate is often tested out first for a trial period of a few weeks to make sure that it works, before being prescribed on a longer-term basis but with regular check-ups. Children may need medication for years, sometimes into adulthood. Sometimes the medicine can be used for phases to allow a child to catch up to a degree educationally and socially, with holiday periods (no medication) in between.

Newer preparations

Methylphenidate is now available in slow-release preparations with only once-a-day dosage, avoiding the embarrassment of taking tablets in school. The dual-release tablet Concerta XL cannot be abused because of its particular slow-release structure. Equasym XL is in the form of a powder in a capsule, so can be suitable for children who cannot swallow tablets.

More recently, atomoxetine (Strattera), which has a similar structure to antidepressants, has become available. Unlike methylphenidate, because it is not a stimulant, it is not a controlled drug. Unlike stimulants that last for the daytime only, it can last for 24 hours, but takes over a month to reach effective levels. It is perhaps less effective for severe ADHD symptoms but often suitable for adolescents who need to avoid risky impulsive behaviours and to study more in the evenings. Its different side-effect profile may also suit some more than others.

Parenting groups

These groups are particularly helpful for parents of children with ADHD who also develop oppositional or conduct problems, because these children particularly need firm, caring and consistent parenting, without which they gravitate towards trouble. The focus is on supporting parents in building a stronger relationship between themselves and their child. Many parents may have given up trying to discipline their children because they never seem to listen anyhow, even if they attended a parenting group before. Once the child is medicated, however, they will then be able to listen, stop, think and learn, so will respond to what hasn't worked before. Building on universal parenting groups, there are now more specialised groups available for parents of children with ADHD in some areas.

Comparison of the new drug, atomoxetine, with stimulants

Characteristic	Stimulants	Atomoxetine
Class of drug	Stimulant (methylphenidate or dexamfetamine)	Non-stimulant (antidepressant structure similar to Prozac)
Legal status	Controlled substance	Not controlled
Duration of action	Effective within 30 minutes	Takes weeks to produce effect
	4 hours (short acting)	24 hours – includes early morning and late afternoon
	8–12 hours (slow-release form)	
Suitability and symptom cover (time of day)	School day cover only	Late night as well (e.g. adolescents)
	Can't cover after 8pm or may cause insomnia	24-hour cover
		May help sleep
Effectiveness	Stronger effect	Less strong effect
Dosing	Can dose flexibly, e.g. drug holidays	Need steady daily dose
Main side effects	Appetite and weight decrease	Appetite and weight decrease
	May temporarily lower mood in some	May help to mellow moody teens but very rare reports of suicidal thoughts
	May worsen epilepsy or tics (care needed)	Raised blood pressure (must check regularly)
	Insomnia	Liver toxicity (very rarely)

Where do I get help?

You will need to be referred by your doctor to a specialist paediatrician or to Child and Adolescent Mental Health Services (CAMHS) for diagnosis and treatment. Some doctors outside mental health services sometimes have expertise in ADHD, but may not offer the wider range of treatments beyond medication for more complicated situations.

Support is available through ADHD support agencies that run parent support groups in most areas, schools (educational psychologists and advice with special needs support) and possibly Social Services (for family support, financial advice or support, or childcare support if relevant).

There are many excellent self-help books on ADHD available, and the ADHD support agencies will provide lists of their preferred ones. Details of all these resources can be found in the chapter 'Useful information' on page 165.

Autism and related disorders

Autism and related disorders are also collectively known as autistic spectrum disorders (ASDs). Autism used to be viewed as a rare condition (affecting fewer than one in 1,000 children). In the last few years, however, there has been a fourfold increase in the diagnosis of autistic spectrum disorders, largely because we are more aware and better able to identify them, especially at the milder end of the spectrum, bringing the figure up to 6 per 1,000 children. Severe autism is often associated with global learning difficulty and epilepsy. Another name often used is pervasive developmental disorder, although this term may also be used to cover a wider range of children with similar problems who do not fit all the criteria for autism. The disorder may range from mild to severe, with varying levels of learning and speech difficulties.

Autism is a developmental brain disorder. It usually starts before the age of three years, often with subtle abnormalities from birth. Children may be severely affected, yet usually look normal. This can be very difficult for parents in public places, where onlookers may stare at a child behaving badly and incorrectly assume that the parents are incompetent or abusive.

Other names for the mild forms are Asperger's syndrome (with no speech delay) and Kanner's syndrome, in which children with normal intelligence find it difficult to relate to others, appearing strange, different and sometimes clumsy.

Although there are reports of autism being linked with the MMR (measles, mumps and rubella) vaccine, extensive research to date has not supported this idea, and your child is probably safer with than without the injection, as these infectious diseases can be very serious. (Outbreaks have occurred where MMR has not been taken up.)

There is no test for autism, and the diagnosis depends on an expert asking very detailed questions about the child's symptoms, behaviour, etc. since the time he was born, getting reports from school, observing the child directly, and getting specialist advice from speech and language and occupational therapists.

Problems with social interaction

Autistic children are often socially awkward and aloof. They live in a world of their own, with restricted and unusual interests. They don't develop the to-and-fro social conversations that most people do, and often avoid eye contact. They often don't understand non-verbal gestures or facial expressions, and often can't work out what other people are thinking and feeling. For this reason, they often lack empathy, responding inappropriately to someone getting hurt, or making naïve and embarrassing remarks. They may have a stilted manner and get easily upset for no understandable reason. They tend not to become attached to parents as normal children do, so they can be very unresponsive.

Communication problems

A child who is severely affected may be unable to talk, whereas one more mildly affected may have strange or stilted speech, with unusual words added, or copying or repeating words in a strange way. A child may tend to take language literally, and use it literally too. Parents can ask 'Go and get the milk', but if they failed to add 'and bring it to me', they could wait forever as the child took the milk elsewhere with him. They also struggle to use non-verbal gesture to communicate (for example, not pointing to what they want but reaching for it instead).

Rituals, routines and rigidity

Autistic children often have to do things in a certain way all the time and cannot cope with change. Deviation from the routine can lead to huge anxiety, upsets and tantrums, extreme withdrawal or refusal to cooperate. This can be understood as the child's way of trying to preserve a sense of sameness and stability in a world that he doesn't understand.

The child may develop rituals and mannerisms such as spinning plates, flicking book pages over and over again or hand flapping when excited. They are often oversensitive to touch, smell, taste and sounds, which can either cause great upsets or be used to soothe them, depending on their individual sensitivities.

Autistic children can't play imaginatively, and tend to line toys up, look at them from an odd angle, or spin, sniff, taste or touch them rather than play 'make believe'. They can often develop isolated obsessional interests in subjects such as cars, trains, numbers or historical topics, and may have exceptional isolated talents despite global learning disability, like the Dustin Hoffmann character in 'Rain man'.

Helping a child with autism

Autistic children have special qualities. They are often unable to lie, may have special talents or interests, and can persist with those tasks that others would tire of much earlier because of their tendency to over-focus or perseverate on the task that fascinates them. The eccentric professor typifies the person with Asperger's syndrome at the high functioning end.

Autistic children usually need a team of specialists to provide the right support. It is important that you ask your GP or health visitor to refer your child to a paediatrician and/or child psychiatrist if you suspect this condition. Early specialist intervention with careful educational planning can make a big difference, with a whole school approach of structure and routine.

Being the parent of an autistic child can be extremely exhausting and demanding, and sometimes bonding between the parents and child is severely affected. Often the child doesn't show affection in the way other children do, which can be very unrewarding for his parents. They may then get demoralised, depressed or withdrawn and therefore, unwittingly, 'emotionally unavailable' to the child who needs this sort of attention more than other children.

Getting an accurate diagnosis with the right support can make a huge difference, especially if this enables you to come to terms with having a handicapped child. In children with autism and ADHD, the tips on pages 94–5 can also be helpful. See the Family Doctor book *Understanding ADHD, Autism, Dyslexia and Dyspraxia* for a further discussion of this subject.

Although most of the management is non-medical, with specialist parent support groups, behavioural measures and school support being particularly helpful, in a clinic for ASD, up to 75% have been found also to have ADHD, which responds to medication as above. Other comorbid conditions must always be identified and treated (for example, epilepsy). When all other measures have been taken in, emerging evidence suggests that low-dose neuroleptics such as risperidone can hugely reduce the extremes of emotion, anxiety and aggression where other measures have failed, and can dramatically improve quality of life. This will need specialist prescribing as referred by your GP, because this medication is licensed for use in severe psychiatric illnesses such as psychosis, but not for autism.

Depression

Most children with behavioural problems are not depressed, although some have both. Depression is quite common, occurring in up to five per cent of children of school age and up to eight per cent of teenagers. Boys and girls are equally affected as children, with more girls than boys affected in adolescence. Depression is often not recognised for what it is and can lead to moodiness, irritability and difficult behaviour that is mistaken for a negative attitude. If it is missed, being told off for a bad attitude will only make matters worse, so it is important to check for this if young people become difficult when previously they were easy going. Only ten per cent of children with depression get referred to a specialist for help, even though the condition is treatable.

Symptoms of depression in children are often vague and come on gradually, so are easy to miss. They include a low mood, lack of enjoyment (often expressed as boredom) and low energy levels – feeling tired all the time, irritability and poor sleep. The child may be anxious too, sometimes with thoughts of suicide or self-harm. Children give up their usual activities and friends, and tend to become quiet, withdrawn and moody. Younger children may also complain of aches and pains, be more clingy and whining, get agitated easily or become fearful and anxious.

Depression has many causes, but is usually the result of a combination of genetic and environmental factors (for example, family history of depression and negative life events).

It is important to be aware of your child's emotional state, and to be supportive if you suspect that she is feeling low. Talk to your child and see if you can identify any triggers or chronic problems such as bullying that you can help her to deal with. If you are aware of these difficulties but feel unable to deal with them yourself, seek help. Your child may be irritated by your questions and not know the reason for her low mood, but you can give her support by listening and indicating that you are there to help. Avoid arguments. See if your child enjoys some activities more than others and, if so, rearrange her timetable with less pressure, more fun, praise and reward. If your child seems depressed for longer than a few weeks, you should consult your GP for specialist help from the Child and Adolescent Mental Health Service (CAMHS). Children often respond to psychological treatments (especially cognitive–behavioural therapy which may be available online for older teenagers and adults), and antidepressants may sometimes be helpful too. See the Family Doctor book *Understanding Depression* for a more detailed discussion of this subject.

Anxiety

Severe anxiety (see page 65), panic attacks, severe phobias (fears), and obsessional and/or compulsive behaviours should be referred via your GP to the CAMHS.

Anxiety itself is unlikely to lead to behavioural problems unless the child is autistic and avoiding change. Nevertheless, some children can display difficult behaviours in relation to anxiety in the following situations.

Separation anxiety

Some children may refuse to go to bed or to school because they fear separation from their parents. This can occur after loss (for example, death of a loved one) or trauma (for example, abuse or bullying), in a child with an anxious temperament, in a child with an insecure attachment to his parents (for example, if the parent was depressed previously) or if the child is physically unwell. Responding with anger and arguments makes the child feel unloved and increases the anxiety about the relationship, making the behaviour worse. This can become a vicious circle. The solution is to have clear limits at bedtime, allowing for quality one-to-one time with the parents, providing reassurance, allowing the child to confide about any worries or problems that can be dealt with, and ignoring further attempts to sustain contact, without arguing. Praise and reward for going to sleep or to school without a fuss will help improve the situation, which usually is outgrown in time.

Some children can be severely traumatised after accidents or abusive experiences, and develop PTSD or post-traumatic stress disorder, which occurs also in adults. They may become tearful, fearful, hypervigilant, withdrawn or irritable, and develop panic attacks. They can get insomnia, nightmares, separation anxiety, bedwetting and flashbacks. All this can present as demanding difficult behaviour if it is not understood for what it is, especially if parents have also been traumatised and are having similar symptoms. It is important to seek early specialist advice from the CAMHS via the GP, or contact the NSPCC (National Society for the Prevention of Cruelty to Children – see page 178) for advice if unsure, because these symptoms are readily treatable with behavioural and talking treatments and, if necessary, medication, and do better if caught early.

Eating disorders

Don't have battles over food. If your child's behaviours around food may become difficult or rigid, be aware of the possibility of eating disorders. If your child's dieting or eating habits restrict her lifestyle, you should seek help from the CAMHS through your GP, because early intervention is associated with a better prognosis. This applies to anorexia (a condition in which a child restricts food, has a fear of fatness, loses weight and has a distorted body image) and to bulimia (an eating disorder characterised by bingeing and vomiting), for which treatment is also available. Children are presenting earlier with these conditions, so it is important to be aware of this and catch it early. Family therapy can often help, especially in younger children where individual work may be more difficult. See the Family Doctor book *Understanding Eating Disorders* for a more detailed discussion of this subject.

KEY POINTS

- If a diagnosis is missed, the child and/or family may be blamed inappropriately

- Many children are often incorrectly labelled as 'naughty'

- 'Bad' behaviour in children may be the result of a medical condition, such as hearing loss, poor eyesight or a chronic illness

- Bad behaviour may be related to underlying neurodevelopmental disorders such as attention deficit hyperactivity disorder or autism that have not been diagnosed, or to mood disorders such as depression and anxiety, that readily respond to treatment if identified in time.

- Attention deficit hyperactivity disorder is more common in the UK than previously thought; it responds well to medication and other treatments and other interventions

- Autism is a rare cause of behavioural problems, but milder forms are more commonly recognised and respond well to whole school interventions

- Neurodevelopmental disorders often exist together with and can be further complicated by depression

- Criticism and blame make most conditions worse

- Praise, support, and firm and consistent discipline improve communication and will help parents and child to cope better

- Most conditions are treatable, or at least benefit from being recognised and understood

- Early detection and intervention are very important to prevent behavioural problems from becoming established, and lead to the best outcomes

Finding solutions to problem behaviour

Understanding the meaning of your child's behaviour
How to work out what's going on

Understanding your child's behaviour is often the key to finding a solution. If you think of most behavioural problems as indicating that your child needs help and attention (*what does he want?*) rather than seeing them as an attack on you (*he's doing this on purpose to wind me up!*), you are more likely to find an answer.

A key to working out the underlying cause is to try to put yourself in your child's shoes and see things from his point of view. One way of getting more insight into this is to think through your child's life up to now, marking down the key life events at different ages and thinking through how they may have impacted on him, including more recent triggers.

By asking certain questions, you can try to understand the meaning of your child's behaviour, identify any possible causes and other underlying problems that may need tackling first, and decide which problem to focus on, so that you can work out what to do. The following questions may give you some clues as to why your child is behaving in this way. They are most likely to be useful if you work on them with a family member or close friend, although you may be able to come up with some answers yourself.

Having another person with whom to talk it through can shed new perspectives and new light on problems, especially if you feel stuck. Family members may have helpful observations that you may be unaware of, and impartial people often see issues that you as a family are too close or negatively biased to notice.

On the other hand, it is important to add that sometimes with some problems it is not possible or even necessary to understand your child's behaviour in order to find solutions. So some therapies are based around finding solutions rather than digging up problems.

Trying different solutions methodically as you would do for a crying baby may be all that is needed, although understanding behaviour can often be helpful to get to the underlying cause of the problem.

Useful questions for understanding behavioural problems
What's the problem?

- What is the problem?
- Whose problem is it?
- Who is the most troubled by the problem?
- Is the problem mainly with the child, or is it someone else's problem?

For example, a stressed mother may think that the

child is the 'problem' as he affects everyone, but these questions may help her to realise that the 'stress' is mostly with her and that she is inadvertently worsening the problem by reacting negatively to her son. She may be the one who needs extra support.

Features of the problem

If the problem lies mainly with the child:

- Is the behaviour normal for this developmental stage?

- Is your child the only one with this problem?

- Where does the behaviour happen – at home, at school or both?

- Is your child with anyone in particular at the time when the problem occurs (or perhaps not with someone in particular)?

- When does the behaviour occur: for example, is it when you and your child are apart, in new situations, at a particular time of day?

- Are there any recognisable triggers such as a lack of sleep the night before, hunger, reminders of an upsetting incident?

- What makes the behaviour worse and what makes it better?

History of the problem

- When did the bad behaviour problem start?

- What was going on leading up to the start of the bad behaviour?

- What are the broader issues to consider? For example, have there been any significant life events, losses or changes in circumstances recently? Have there been any family or school changes? Are you or other family members more stressed than usual? Are there any other family tensions around? Could your child be noticing this? Have you talked to your child about what's going on? Would it help if you did? If not, would it help if someone outside the family did? If any of these issues are relevant, you may be better off focusing your energies on resolving these difficulties rather than on your child's behaviour.

- Has anyone in the family had similar problems ever? If so, what helped? Was there an underlying health problem?

Vulnerability factors

Was your child vulnerable in any way before the problem started (for example, is he significantly different from his peers in any way – does he have any learning difficulties or physical illnesses or is he socially isolated)?

Positive parenting strategies – are they in place?

- Are you paying attention to your child's bad behaviour and ignoring his good behaviour? If so, make sure that you ignore bad behaviour where possible and attend to good behaviour.

- Do you and your partner agree on which approaches to try? Are you working together or against each other? Be consistent.

- Have you tried any solutions? Have you been consistent in what you have tried? Don't give up too soon.

- Does your reaction to your child remain constant despite your mood? Are there times when your style is more effective than other times? What is different about the times when you are more effective? Can you do this more often? Firmness, consistency, praise and clear instructions work better than hostility and blame. Be aware of your reactions to your child. Keep firm and positive regardless of your mood.

- What are your thoughts and feelings about your child? Are they positive or negative? Which thoughts help you be a better parent? How about trying to notice and remember the helpful thoughts, for times when the unhelpful ones interfere with your parenting. Write yourself reminders of what works.

Positive unexpected outcomes and possible solutions

Are there any times when you would have expected this behaviour and it didn't happen? If so, what was different? Can you re-create this difference and, if so, how? Is there any pattern to the times when the behaviour never arises? Can anything be learned from this that may help? There are bound to be exceptions to bad behaviour. Learn from them and apply them to recreate a positive atmosphere.

Family support

- We can all support people by listening to them, understanding them emotionally, or physically helping them, and praising rather than criticising. Look after each other and be less critical.

- Is anyone in the family feeling unsupported in any way? If so, who? In what way? Who feels this most? Again, support each other. Rather than criticise, what can you do to help?

How to keep an ABC behaviour monitoring diary

It may help to record your child's behaviour for a while using a diary.

If you want a fuller picture, you can record three main types of information in separate columns in addition to a column for time and place.

Antecedents (A)

These are the events that led up to the behaviour.

If you have any idea of what your child was thinking and feeling at the time, it helps to record this (you can ask him this after the event).

Behaviour (B)

What did your child do?

How long did this last?

How severe was it (out of 10)?

Consequences (C)

What happened afterwards?

What did you do?

What effect did this have?

Date	Day	Time	Antecedents (A)	Behaviour (B)	Consequences (C)
23/06/03	Monday	17.30	James' younger brother playing with James' toys	James hit brother (4/10)	I shouted at him and sent him to his bedroom. He said this was not fair and didn't talk to us for an hour after.

- Do you all feel listened to? Or do you need more time to listen to each other? If so, can this be done safely without criticism? Would it help if you found time for private one-to-one conversations between any two family members? Make time to have conversations in which you can really listen to and understand each other.

- Would more support of any sort be helpful? If so, what sort of support would be the most helpful? Who could best provide this support and how? What is the first step towards making this happen? Get the support you need.

- It helps to think widely and laterally about alternatives if the support you think you need is not available, for example, if there is no special needs teacher for your son's problem, could you contact the local training college and ask the tutors if any students training in special needs could provide some support as part of their work experience? Use all the resources in your community, beyond your immediate family if necessary.

Keeping a diary

If you need more information and feel in the dark, it may help to keep a diary and monitor your child's behaviour for a while (see pages 114–15). You should record particularly good behaviour as well as bad, and rate the frequency (how many times in an hour or day?) as well as the severity of each event (marks out of 10?).

Identify in your diary the place and time of any episodes of particularly good or bad behaviour. The ratings can be helpful in monitoring any change in behaviour if you try any potential solutions, and can

Example of an ABC behaviour monitoring diary

This example was used to monitor jealousy between a brother and his younger sister.

SATURDAY AM
Antecedents
We were having lunch. Max had had a bad day and we were in a rush. Jane (his sister) was singing to herself.

Behaviour
Max kicked Jane (5/10).

Consequences
We yelled at him and comforted Jane. He accused us of taking her side and then had a tantrum for half an hour (8/10).

Example of an ABC behaviour monitoring diary (contd)

SATURDAY PM
Antecedents
I read Max a story
and we had a chat.

Behaviour
Max played nicely
with Jane for half an
hour.

Consequences
We praised them
both for playing
together nicely and
they were pleased.

Example of an ABC behaviour monitoring diary (contd)

SUNDAY AM
Antecedents
Max had been doing his homework which he finds difficult. Jane was singing.

Behaviour
Max kicked Jane (5/10).

Consequences
We told him calmly to apologise or go to his room. Jane was comforted and asked to play quietly.

Example of an ABC behaviour monitoring diary (contd)

SUNDAY PM
Antecedents
We offered to help Max with his homework, after which we'd all go to the park.

Behaviour
Max did his homework willingly.

Consequences
We all went out to the park as we'd promised.

Example of an ABC behaviour monitoring diary (contd)

Observations/notes

- High stress situations lead to problems – Jane singing often triggers rows. Why is Jane singing? Is she stressed, too?

- Is she aware of doing this?

- Losing our temper makes tantrums worse.

- Setting limits calmly before everyone gets too upset helps.

- I've noticed that Max goes quiet before he loses his temper.

- Praise and rewards for good behaviour help.

Plan

- Will try to get teatime help from family, older siblings or a babysitter on busy nights, or else will cook earlier in the day or fix an easy meal.

- Will have a chat with children about rewards for being kind to each other – must agree these with partner. Will praise and reward children for kindness to each other.

- Will ask Jane if she's noticed Max going quiet before the storm, and if she noticed a pattern between her singing and his kicking.

- Will ask her to be less noisy when we're eating and when he is trying to study.

- Will try to notice Max going quiet and will praise him for 'sitting quietly' before he loses his temper. This will also remind Jane not to sing!

help you to distinguish mild from severe episodes. You could ask other people such as teachers or relatives to contribute to this exercise and then compare notes.

If identifying problem behaviour in a diary does not help, you could try a 'sparkling moments' diary instead. This is described on page 124.

Tolerating not knowing

It is not always possible to understand why your child behaves as he does. If you insist on knowing why, you can make things much worse, because your child may not be able to verbalise what he wants to say or simply may not be able to work it out himself. Sometimes there isn't an answer to 'why', because there are too many small factors for any single one to be 'the reason'.

Even if you don't know why your child is behaving in this manner, you may still be able to identify what helps and work towards solutions.

Problem-solving

Once you have answers to some of the above questions, you can start finding solutions to any problems that exist. Sometimes it is relatively straightforward: bullying can be stopped, a physical illness can be treated or extra help can be provided for a learning difficulty. Perhaps you are burned out or over-stressed.

If you feel overwhelmed by negative thoughts and feelings, you may need to take time out to calm down and cheer yourself up or get help to challenge some of your negative thoughts. If this doesn't work it may be because you are unable to cope and depressed without being aware of it. This is extremely common. Help is available that can make all the difference.

Prioritising problems

If there are so many problems that you feel overwhelmed and don't know where to start, it may help to make a list in the order of which is bothering you the most to the least. This often helps clarify your thoughts. Don't tackle them all at once. Decide to work on one or two of the problems to start with, and start with those that are easiest to change. This alone can boost your confidence. Plan to pick the others up one at a time. Pace yourself and reward yourself after each step with a break or a small treat.

For those problems that you can't change, you can decide either to learn to live with them or to escape from them if possible. For problems you can't escape from, such as coming to terms with a disability in yourself or your child, taking time to discuss their impact on you can help you cope. Meeting other people with the same problem can also help. You may need to learn to live with the problem rather than fight against it.

Finding solutions

Sometimes we can become so bogged down with problems that we cannot see the wood for the trees when using logical approaches such as those above, and end up the worse for trying. Complex or difficult problems do not always have complex solutions.

Pick the worst problem that you're stuck with. Imagine waking up one morning to a miracle; your problem was gone. How could you tell it was gone? Can you paint a picture of what life would look like without the problem? What would you be doing? What would be different about your child? What would be different about you? What would your relationships be like? What comments would other parents or teachers be making?

You can also do this part of the exercise with your child. Tell him to imagine he was in a time travel machine, travelling to a time in the future where the problem had gone. Ask him to describe in detail what you would be like as a family, and what you would be doing.

How could you or he make elements of your picture happen here and now? For example, having more one-to-one time, ask your child the same question.

Try to find exceptions to the problem, and describe a time, however brief (a sparkling moment), when the problem was not there.

Try to identify as many of these sparkling moments as possible. You will then realise that some of the 'miracle' is already happening. Have you noticed what makes these moments last longer, or what makes them shorter?

To help you identify this, you can make a 'sparkling moments' diary with your child, in which you both record all his good behaviours. You could also include ratings out of 10 for improvements in behaviour. This can be linked to a reward system of stickers or tokens. You could add photos or other memorabilia to make up a book of evidence of better times happening for you both. This can be very encouraging for you both – a document of all your sparkling moments. Take time to review the book together every day, and share it with other family members.

Recognising the positive

Now that you are more tuned into positive change, what positive changes have you noticed in the last two weeks? You are bound to have noticed what has got worse, but did you spot the improvements? Some things are bound to have got better even if other things got worse. How were they possible? What could you do to increase the likelihood of this happening more often?

Are you aware of your role in making these improvements happen? Most parents fail to notice improvements and, even if they do find them, see change as being caused by others, as they usually feel so helpless about the problems. If you look closely, however, you will notice that the times your child has behaved better are bound to coincide with times when you have given the child extra time, set clearer limits, been more consistent, shouted less, etc.

- What might your child have noticed that was different about you?
- What would be different about you in the sparkling moment?

Once you realise the influence that you do have over your child's behaviour, you can create more of the times when you are in control. The next section gives a detailed account of parenting practices that make a difference. They are bound to coincide with the ones that you notice about yourself when times are good.

Practical parenting tips
Avoid criticism and blame
As discussed, criticism and blame are often destructive forces that lead only to further difficulties and misery. The key to avoiding these is to judge the behaviour, not the child. Instead of saying 'you are bad', it is much more constructive to say 'hitting is bad'. The child can do something about hitting but cannot become a different person.

Practical parenting tips

Sam is seen as trouble. When people see him, they think 'here comes trouble'. All the troubles are seen as brought on by Sam's will, and intentionally done to upset people. This makes people cross with Sam, and Sam cross with them.

However, we can separate Sam from trouble, and make space for Sam to talk to his parents about how they can work together to get rid of trouble. They can identify together what makes trouble worse, and what makes it better, so that they can all work together to reduce trouble, for example, by keeping a sparkling moments diary, or by being 'trouble detectives' together, and 'catching trouble out'.

Solutions may involve Sam having more structured activities to keep him out of trouble, more fun with his parents, being shouted at less, and getting rewards for good behaviour, for example. This sort

Practical parenting tips (contd)

of understanding can take the criticism and blame out of difficult situations, and help the family find new solutions.

Use 'THE' magic word
Talk about THE trouble, THE temper, THE bad behaviour, THE PROBLEM, rather than using 'YOU' language, which personalises things. (How can we fix THE trouble together? rather than why did YOU do it?)

Dealing with behavioural problems
Many strategies are effective at preventing and managing behavioural problems and in improving positive behaviour and relationships in families. There is well-researched evidence that parents and teachers can shape good behaviour in children, using the behavioural strategies described in the next section. The good news is that, by changing your behaviour as parents, even if your child also has a medical problem such as attention deficit hyperactivity disorder (see page 85), you can strongly influence his behaviour and self-esteem.

The earlier you start, the better: these practices are most helpful if you start them when your child is young and continue them consistently throughout her childhood and teenage years. You won't get instant success, so don't be put off if the first thing you try doesn't work or if things get worse before they get better. You should persist for at least about two weeks before moving on to a different approach. Even if it doesn't work, you should keep assessing your child's behaviour, perhaps talking it through with a trusted friend or partner, thinking up new possibilities and trying out different strategies. If you get stuck, don't give up – ask for help. There are many parenting groups available today that show you how to apply these strategies, allow you to discuss real live examples and allow you to share experiences.

How to encourage and develop good behaviour

Build a positive relationship

When you build your relationship with your child, it's like putting money into the bank. You will be able to make withdrawals by asking things of your child as long as you keep putting money in. Criticism, hostility and shouting will all drain the bank account without any returns. If the bank account is empty, there will be nothing to draw on and your child won't cooperate.

There are many ways to build a positive relationship with your child. Play has a vital role in a child's development, and it is important to play with your child without taking over. With regular child-centred play, you will be making deposits in the bank account every time. With an older child, having some private one-to-one time once or twice a week can pay huge dividends, as long as it is based on you being there for your child to meet his needs and wishes rather than to gratify yours. Take time to have fun together.

Your child needs plenty of praise to build up her self-esteem and to enable her to believe she is a good and capable person. Every time you praise her, you build up the bank account. To ensure that your child learns what good behaviour is, you must be specific about what you are praising her for (for example, 'You wiped the table without even being asked, and you remembered to put the cloth back. Well done! You're a real help!').

Show your pleasure physically as well as verbally – a cuddle or pat on the head can be much more powerful than words. Parents associate cuddles and kisses with small children, but older children also need physical touch to feel wanted and loved (although not in front

Tips to build self-esteem in your child

- Start early in his life
- Notice good behaviour
- Focus your attention on what your child can rather than what he can't do
- Remember that no child is perfect, but every child has huge untapped potential
- Remember that your child has unique gifts and talents, even if you cannot see them at the moment
- Praise regularly and specifically
- Make special time together
- Show affection
- Remember: a cuddle and a tickle can go a long way
- Have a good laugh regularly
- Avoid hostility and blame
- Set clear limits
- Set achievable goals
- Give clear commands
- Reward good behaviour
- Inspire and motivate
- Listen to your child
- Treat him with respect
- Be consistent
- Remember that you are your child's role model:
  believe in yourself
  look after yourself
  stop and think
  be positive
- Share good times together
- Play and have fun
- Celebrate his and your achievements together

Robinson Family Star Chart

Date: July

Sarah (age 9)	1	2	3	4	5	6	7	8	9	10	11	etc. for days in the month
Tidy room	✓	✓	✓	✓	✓		✓	✓	✓			
Home on time	✓	✓	✓		✓	✓	✓	✓	✓			
Helping with washing up	✓	✓	✓			✓			✓			
Empty rubbish							✓					
No fights				✓	✓	✓						
Homework done	✓	✓			✓	✓	✓	✓				
Sit still at dinner table	✓	✓		✓	✓	✓	✓	✓	✓			
TOTAL	5	5	3	3	5	5	5	4	4			

Key
Twenty ✓s = One Silver Star
Forty ✓s = One Gold Star

of their friends!). Small gestures of affection make a big difference.

Teach good behaviour

Give your child positive rather than negative attention. For example, try noticing and commenting on what your child does right rather than what he does wrong, especially if he has behavioural problems. Children need attention, and surprisingly prefer negative attention to none. This, however, drains the account.

Reinforce your child's good behaviour by giving him rewards and praise. This is much more effective than punishments. Ignore bad behaviour, even in testing situations, although you may have to set limits in dangerous situations, and be clear and consistent about what you expect.

Star charts and reward systems often work well, even with older children. Work out a system that your child will be interested in. Younger children need immediate visible and practical rewards such as stickers, whereas

Reward good behaviour

- Young children need immediate tangible rewards
- Make rewards age appropriate
- Ignore bad behaviour
- Set limits
- Do not succumb to bribes (when you give in to your child's demands for the sake of peace)

older ones can earn points towards a desired object or outing. Some of the best rewards are free – for example, special one-to-one time with you or your partner, special outings, an extra bedtime story or extra time on the computer or TV. Link the good behaviour with the reward (for example, 'I would like you to wash up, please. *When* you've washed up, *then* you can have a story').

Set limits
Children need to know the limits and learn to live within them. You have to teach your child what is right and wrong, safe and unsafe, allowed and not allowed and have clear, pre-agreed consequences for negative behaviour.

Be clear
When you are telling your child what to do, you need to keep it short and clear, making one request at a time. Shouting 'Stop being naughty' is unclear, but saying in a calm voice 'Please sit still' is more effective. Be positive and polite and be realistic in your demands, and give your child time to respond. Give your child warning of commands – 'You have five more minutes to play and then it's tidy up time'.

Rules

- Be clear about your house rules and make sure everyone else in the household is clear about them too

- Make sure that the adults all buy into these, and are consistent in rewarding compliance with them

- Don't have too many rules, just a few important ones, and be lenient on less important ones; for example, no TV before homework, but it is OK to make a den under the dining room table as long as it is cleaned up on Sunday evening

- Be prepared to negotiate rules with older children and listen to what is important to them

- Agree in advance the consequences of breaching the rules, and make sure everyone including babysitters and grandparents knows them and is prepared to carry them out. For example: 'When a friend sleeps over, if you are not both quiet after 10, you get moved to separate rooms or the friend gets taken home.'

- To be clear about the rules, it is important to distinguish which are the important ones and which are less vital, so that you are not constantly saying 'no'

If your child won't cooperate

Don't lose your temper. Take time out to think and calm down before raising your voice. You may need to shout, but be sure that you know why this is necessary in this instance: for example, if your child is about to run across the road. Shouting is usually a sign that you have lost your cool. Just ignoring your child's bad behaviour may be enough if he is safe, especially if you praise good behaviour as soon as the bad behaviour stops.

With younger children, distraction can work wonders. Set up a constructive alternative activity. For example, if your toddler is whining for sweets, bring out his favourite story book or toy, and attract his attention to this instead.

Plan what you will do if there is a clear breach of pre-agreed rules. Agree the consequence with your child and follow it through. Carry out the loss of privilege without showing any anger, and make quite sure that your child understands why you are doing what you are doing.

Give her ample warning before applying consequences: for example, 'If your toys are not put away in five minutes, X will happen', and make sure the consequences fit the 'crime'. Don't use idle threats and always be consistent.

Make sure that your child understands what she did wrong and what you expect her to do instead. Try to phrase things positively rather than negatively ('when you tidy up you can have a treat', instead of 'if you don't tidy up, you will be sent to your room').

Time out can be very effective when the atmosphere gets heated, as it allows everyone to calm down. You can send your child to another room, with instructions to come out when he is ready to apologise and put things right. Until this happens, you can withdraw certain privileges. For young children, it is not appropriate to do this for long periods of time and, as a rough rule of thumb, not longer in minutes than twice their age, ideally. Time out can be combined with the approach discussed earlier to reduce blame. Don't just tell your child to go away – he will feel rejected. Tell him to go to another room and come back when he's able to leave the 'trouble' behind. This way he gets the message that it's the trouble that you want to be rid of, not him.

Regain control

If you are in a crisis and feel that you are losing control, the best thing you can do is to ask for help. A supportive partner, family member or friend can often step in and take the tension out of the situation by allowing you time out, giving your child positive attention and reminding you and your child that neither of you is to blame.

It can be very helpful to talk things through yourself. 'OK, so I'm feeling angry and fed up. Maybe I'll just take a few minutes to relax first, and then decide what to do when I'm ready. She's just testing me. It's normal. All mothers get tested like this. The job is to stay calm. I'll do that first and take my time. I'll make a plan and stick to it. I can do it.' Remind yourself that you have a number of options that work and decide what to try next.

Work out options and consequences for your child, and present them to him clearly and calmly. 'I want you to stay quietly in bed until you fall asleep. If you go to sleep quietly, you can watch your favourite TV programme tomorrow. For every extra noise tonight, it is 10 minutes off your programme. Good night.' After that, don't get involved in conversations, but praise him as soon as he has been quiet for a few minutes, and remind him that he will get to watch his favourite programme tomorrow. You can also do this by commenting aloud to another person within earshot of your child that you are really impressed with how he went straight to sleep and will ensure that he gets his

When things seem to be getting on top of you

In all situations, try to stay calm and think about what is going on.

- How are you feeling?
- Why are you feeling that way?
- Do you just need a rest?
- Are you really upset with the kids or is it something else that's making you miserable? If so, resolve not to take it out on them but to get help to deal with it elsewhere.
- Have you both got into a shouting match? If so, you may both need time out.
- Are you attending to bad behaviour and ignoring good behaviour?
- What would happen if you ignored this child and went and praised the brother or sister who is behaving well?
- Remind yourself of your child's position: 'How does she see this? Is she upset about something else? Have I listened to her?'
- Remind yourself of times when you managed similar situations. Would these work now?
- Challenge some of your unhelpful beliefs, for example, you are not a failure as a parent if you have had a stressful day and lost your temper. We all have times like this.
- Take time to calm down – have a cup of tea, walk outside briefly or turn some music on.
- Remind yourself of your strengths.
- Make a plan and stick to it, so that you can regain some control.

just rewards. If he is noisy, let him know how much TV is deducted at regular intervals and, if necessary, impose stricter sanctions. Don't get caught up in arguments.

Challenge any negative thoughts you may have. 'I'm a hopeless parent, he's a bad boy, he's doing it to upset me on purpose, he'll grow up into a monster at this rate!' Rather than blame him and yourself, challenge these unhelpful thoughts and replace them with better ones, visualising yourself as the sort of parent you want to become and your child as the sort of child you want him to become.

> 'I may not be perfect, but no one is and I just need to be good enough.'

> 'I'll do this better if I take time out to get a hold on my temper, and stay calm.'

> 'All kids need to learn limits, and they all push them.'

> 'He's not bad. If I teach him clear limits, he'll learn to behave better.'

> 'He's bound to test me at first.'

> 'I'm sure if we discuss this calmly, we'll come up with a solution.'

> 'I can get help if I need it and, with this, we'll get to where we want to be.'

Remind yourself that things may get worse before they get better, but that this approach works after two to three months or sooner if kept up consistently.

Preventive approaches

If your child is prone to bad behaviour, you can stop further problems developing. Be clear and consistent and be prepared for testing after you set limits. Above

Be consistent when dealing with your child

all, listen to your child, offer help and advice when asked for it, and respect her needs and level of understanding. Anticipate problems and work out solutions in advance. Set up rewards for positive behaviour at a time when you are likely to be busy: for example, 'If you play quietly while I'm on the phone, you can have a treat'. This is not a bribe, but a well-earned reward that you set up in advance. A bribe is when you give in to your child's demands for the sake of peace, which only reinforces the bad behaviour. Your child is not automatically entitled to video games, mobile phones, etc. If he has these and other treats, make sure that they are earned by him for good behaviour, and monitored accordingly with access conditional on behaviour.

Look after yourself and give yourself time off. Take time to develop supportive relationships with your partner, friends and family.

Parental consistency is important. If you say 'no' and your partner says 'yes', your child will be confused and more likely to persist until he gets his own way. When children don't listen, or disobey, it is often not because they are naughty, but because they have learned that they can usually get what they want if they are persistent enough.

The best way to train your child to whine, nag, argue or be aggressive is to give in occasionally to this behaviour. It teaches him to persist even harder. Although it is extremely difficult, being firm from the start will make the future much easier for you all.

Parental separation or divorce
Marital breakdown is increasingly common and upsetting to everyone. Children may feel a great sense

Dealing with your child's behaviour problem

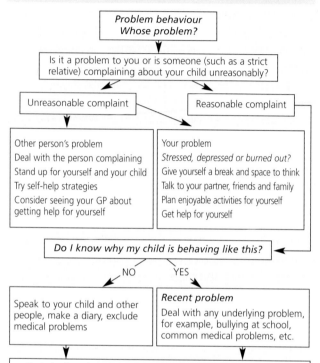

Problem behaviour
Whose problem?

Is it a problem to you or is someone (such as a strict relative) complaining about your child unreasonably?

Unreasonable complaint

Reasonable complaint

Other person's problem
Deal with the person complaining
Stand up for yourself and your child
Try self-help strategies
Consider seeing your GP about getting help for yourself

Your problem
Stressed, depressed or burned out?
Give yourself a break and space to think
Talk to your partner, friends and family
Plan enjoyable activities for yourself
Get help for yourself

Do I know why my child is behaving like this?

NO   YES

Speak to your child and other people, make a diary, exclude medical problems

Recent problem
Deal with any underlying problem, for example, bullying at school, common medical problems, etc.

Try behavioural management strategies, for example, star charts

Long-standing problem
Don't blame yourself or your child – join together to fight the 'trouble'
Try behavioural management strategies (for example, star charts)
Try to approach this systematically with support from a partner, friend or group
Consider joining a local parenting or other support group

If the problem persists, is extreme or very worrying
Consult your GP, health visitor, school nurse or teacher
Ask to be referred to a specialist if necessary, for example, the Child and Adolescent Mental Health Service (CAMHS)

of loss, abandonment, rejection, insecurity, anger and guilt, especially if they think their difficult behaviour contributed to the situation.

This is made much worse if the parents use the children as go-betweens, are openly critical of each other, ask the child to take sides or be critical of the other parent, use his affection as a weapon against one another or expect the child to look after the parent (supporting the parent through their upset, and perhaps feeling unable to express their own feelings in case it upsets the parent too much).

Sometimes a separated or divorced parent may try to buy the child's affection by showering him with gifts or treats. This makes it impossible for the other parent to manage, especially if he or she is in financial difficulty, and harms the child's relationship with the parent who can't compete. If you are in this situation, remember that your child needs you both, so this approach ultimately damages your child rather than your ex-partner.

In any case, most children see through bribes. Parental conflict makes them feel torn in two, having to take sides, and ultimately prevents them from getting the love and attention that they need from each parent. The inconsistency often leads to behavioural problems.

Although nearly half the children in this country see their parents split up, most cope extremely well. This is much more likely to be the case when parents continue to work together to provide a consistent loving environment for their child, regardless of the fact that they no longer love each other. This is feasible and works. However acrimonious the split, if you are in this position, as long as you have the overriding goal of wanting the best for your children, you can achieve this by:

- Being open, talking to your child and answering her questions
- Reassuring your child
- Telling her you both still love her and will care for her
- Although you take her views into account, you as parents will still be jointly making the decisions
- Being reliable about your arrangements to see your child
- Carrying on with as normal, busy and undisrupted a routine as possible
- Getting outside support, for example, mediation, if you and your ex cannot see eye to eye on childcare issues.
- Allow your child access to talk to someone unbiased outside the family in whom they can confide

KEY POINTS

- If a diagnosis is missed, the child and/or family may be blamed inappropriately

- It is often helpful to work out what is causing your child's bad behaviour, possibly with the help of a close friend or teacher

- It can help to keep a diary and monitor your child's behaviour over a certain period of time

- Separate the person from the bad behaviour

- Once you have an idea of the cause, you can try some solutions, such as using the self-help strategies outlined above

- It is important to build a positive relationship with your child and bolster his self-esteem. You also need to teach your child good behaviour, set realistic limits and be consistent

- It always helps to avoid criticism and blame, although you must be firm about setting limits on behaviour

- Look for sparkling moments and use 'THE' language and join him in finding solutions together

- Get help if you do not succeed

- Remember that you can have a huge positive impact as a parent – you can make a difference; it's never too late

Surviving parenthood

Your life situation, behaviour and mood can affect your child's behaviour. If you are in a bad mood, perhaps because of a difficult life situation, you are more likely to be irritable towards your child, and think negatively of him, setting off a pattern of negative interactions, criticism and hostility. It is important to deal with your own needs and emotions, as well as those of your child so that you feel better, have the capacity to enjoy your child more, and can develop a good secure relationship together.

Self-awareness

It is crucial to be self-aware; this means being in touch with your deepest wishes, emotions and beliefs. This will enable you to achieve the right balance between giving what you can and getting what you need. Parents often put their own needs last, and feel guilty if they don't give all their attention to their children. If you had a bad day and take it out on your children, they will respond with bad behaviour that makes your bad day even worse. You may find, however, that if you are able to stop and think about your bad day, calm yourself down with a five-minute treat (such as a walk, sitting down with a cup of tea, a biscuit or a magazine, having a shower or calling a friend) and then respond positively to your children's demands, they will respond positively back to you, which may then turn your bad day into a good one. The atmosphere at home then feels better.

Listen to yourself
You have to listen to your body, mind and, in particular, emotions to work out what you really want to do, and take time to think. This can help guide you to the best course of action and will help you get the balance right. The more you listen to what you really need, the happier you are, the more positive you can be and the more confident and resilient you become.

Negative thoughts or feelings
Negative emotions are not always bad, for example, if you are in a situation where you keep getting hurt and wonder why you keep feeling exhausted and hopeless, maybe you need to get away from the pain, rather than kid yourself that 'things will get better'.

However, negative feelings can also be very destructive and damaging if you don't keep them in check. They can lead to negative and unhelpful thoughts. You may become convinced that you are hopeless or useless, and avoid facing life because of anxiety and a fear of failure or may feel as if you literally 'fall apart' under stress.

If you believe you are a lousy parent with horrible monstrous children, you will see no point in trying to be a good parent, and will get short-term gratification from shouting at 'the monsters who asked for it'. Negative beliefs, in this way, can become self-fulfilling prophecies.

Negative thoughts and beliefs are just that. Thoughts and beliefs. They do not represent the truth about who you are. The truth or evidence about what you really are like lies with what you actually do, rather than what you think. If you resist or fight these negative beliefs, and choose to believe in yourself, you can change your behaviour accordingly, to be how you prefer to be and become whatever you want to become. You can distract yourself from negative thoughts by doing something positive such as exercise or phoning a friend.

If you find it difficult to cope or to believe in yourself, it may help to talk with close confidant(e)s about your thoughts and feelings, problems and relationships both past and present. If you identify significant difficulties that you can't resolve informally, voluntary agencies, counsellors, your GP and other professional agencies are valuable sources of help.

Positive thinking

It always helps to remind yourself of positive things in your life that you feel grateful for, to get yourself in a better frame of mind. To fight negative (unhelpful) thoughts and feelings, you can keep a list of positive (helpful) ones to replace them with. You could practise singing or repeating comforting thoughts and sayings, replacing 'I can't do it' with 'I can do it with the right help, in time', 'I'll be OK', 'It's all going fine, according to plan', 'If I keep trying, I'll get there', 'There is enough help out there, and if I keep asking for it, it will come in time'.

You could also keep visual prompts of your success around you, pin up photos of happier times, keep a file of all your certificates of achievement or a diary of your successes and stick notes up around the house with your favourite comforting sayings. Imagine getting where you want to be. Imagine the small steps along the way and visualise each one. Keep it realistic. You can practise this as you go about your daily activities. This will help you believe in yourself.

Depression

Depression is extremely common, especially among women with young children, affecting up to one in four people in their lifetime. There is increasing evidence that maternal depression, especially if it is long lasting, is associated with behavioural difficulties in children.

What causes it?

Depression is often triggered by negative stresses and life events such as the loss of a close relative. Some women experience postnatal depression after the birth of a baby. You are more likely to get depressed if you have a family history of depression, if you have experienced many losses in the past – especially if you lost your mother in childhood – or if you are under a lot of stress. Parents can get run-down and depressed, and research suggests that you are at higher risk for this if you have three or more children under five at home and no paid employment outside the home, especially if you have little support from others.

How do I tell if I've got depression?

The symptoms of depression vary from person to person and can be difficult to identify. You are likely to be depressed if you constantly feel run-down and exhausted to the extent that most things feel like a huge effort. You may also have disturbed sleep, wake up feeling unrefreshed, suffer from a low mood – especially in the mornings – and don't enjoy or look forward to things that used to cheer you up and/or have constant negative and critical thoughts about yourself, for example, feeling like a burden to those around you.

Anxiety symptoms may make you indecisive as well. Depression can distort your belief systems and convince you that you are hopeless and useless. Other symptoms include tearfulness, irritability and poor concentration. If you have always suffered from low self-esteem and similar symptoms, you may have dysthymia, a milder more chronic (long-lasting) form of depression, which can become complicated by depression – so-called 'double depression'.

So what can be done about it?

First, do not blame yourself or view yourself as a failure – this is typical depressive thinking that stops you getting help. If you think you may be depressed, you could ask your GP or health visitor for advice. Any treatment will benefit not only you but also your children, who are acutely sensitive to your mood. Your children will be more likely to play up and develop behavioural problems if they sense that you are not yourself.

Treatments for depression are very effective and have few side effects. The main treatments are antidepressants or cognitive–behavioural therapy. Neither of these will solve the problems that may have triggered the depression in the first place, but both will enable you to deal with the stress more efficiently. The more you can identify the cause of stress and deal with it, the better. You are likely to remain depressed if you can't find ways of improving your situation.

Cognitive–behavioural therapy (CBT) is a talking treatment that helps you to 'recharge your batteries' by doing more fun activities in your spare time, increasing your activity levels and identifying and challenging unhelpful thoughts. A psychologist, psychiatrist or psychotherapist or other mental health worker can offer you CBT, but this involves investing regular time and commitment to the therapy.

Antidepressants such as Prozac (fluoxetine) are safe with few side effects and are non-addictive. Side effects are usually mild and transient, but vary depending on the antidepressant. There is now such a wide choice available that you can usually find one that suits you, if you are prepared to persist for a while. Your GP can prescribe these medicines. There is increasing evidence that St John's wort, a herbal remedy, can be as effective as an antidepressant, and this is a common alternative used in Germany. However, you should not take St John's wort without medical advice, especially if you take any other medication or have a chronic medical condition, because St John's wort has similar ingredients to Prozac in it, but in an unquantified dose, and may interact badly with other substances. You never know exactly what is put into herbal preparations, as they are not monitored and regulated in the same way as medicines are. Whatever you choose, it is best to be monitored by someone who knows about the medicines so that you can be sure of taking them at the right dose.

Anger

It's common to feel angry from time to time when things aren't going as planned. However, constant anger can take over your life in a similar way to depression.

Some people who have been badly treated in life feel hard done by and angry at their predicament. People who are angry all the time have difficulty relaxing and enjoying things, and often survive by losing their temper. This may help in the short term, but, in the long term, it can lead to relationship problems, more conflict, more marital discord and more violence. In turn, this often leads to behavioural problems in children by setting a negative role model for children who learn to copy such behaviour. This can lead to inconsistent and harsh parenting and can also be associated with more child abuse.

Some people who feel very angry much of the time find alcohol provides short-term relief, but this can result in addiction, leading to problems with work and relationships and the breakdown of the family. Alcohol also unleashes violent behaviour and makes people more depressed in the long term.

Anger management

If you find that you get angry regularly, there are several ways to control your temper. If you take time to work out what you are really angry and upset about rather than the immediate trigger, which may be something trivial like being stuck in a traffic jam, you may find that just talking about it helps. Sometimes, anger covers other upset feelings that have been buried from the past. Reopening these may be painful but also helpful, because it may be possible to do something constructive about the situation that is upsetting you. For example, if you had harsh or abusive parents and feel angry about this, you may find that you suppress this, only to unwittingly take out this anger on those around you, leading to further hostile relationships with those you are closest to, further fuelling your anger. In this instance, psychotherapy, counselling, meditation or spiritual work may be helpful to you.

Some people diffuse anger by using energy constructively, by making jokes, by diverting it into creative projects or by doing a lot of exercise.

If the situation is out of your control, you are probably best off finding other situations where you can have more of an influence. For example, if you are not being promoted in your job despite your best efforts, perhaps you could try a different job, or develop a creative outlet instead of staying in a situation that makes you feel helpless. Exercise and avoiding too much stress can also be very helpful, because this will make you feel better about yourself and more able to enjoy things that don't make you angry. You may need to seek help from a therapist through your GP if these strategies are not effective.

KEY POINTS

■ Your behaviour and mood can affect your child's behaviour

■ Depression is treatable and is not a sign of failure

■ Parental depression can lead to behavioural and emotional problems in their children

■ If you feel depressed, it is important to seek help and look after yourself

■ Anger in parents can destroy family relationships, negatively affects children's behaviour and needs to be kept under control

■ Alcohol makes things worse

■ You are your children's role model, and they will learn your behaviours

■ Looking after yourself will make you a happier person and a better parent

Where do I go for help?

To work out what's normal and what isn't, people who know your child and whom you trust will be able to give you an idea, especially teachers and other experienced parents. However, if people reassure you that your child is fine but you are still not sure, you can ask to be referred to an expert for an opinion.

School-related problems

If the problem is school related, your child's school will have a procedure that you can follow to get help. You usually, in the first instance, report the problem to your child's teacher and try to work on it together. If this fails, you can then involve the special educational needs coordinator (SENCO) at the school, who should offer his or her expertise and devise an educational plan.

All schools should have a SENCO. If the plan fails or is not forthcoming, the school can arrange an appointment for an outside expert or educational psychologist to see your child. You can also request this yourself from the educational authorities, through the education offices, which are usually in your town hall. An educational psychologist is a psychologist who has also done teacher training and been a teacher. He or she has great expertise in learning difficulties and school-related behavioural problems, but may have less experience of clinical/medical problems.

Schools should also be able to put you in touch with educational welfare officers (EWOs) if your child is refusing to go to school. If you are unhappy with the school's response, there is a parent adviser in the educational offices of most town halls who can provide advice and support.

Underlying disorders

If you suspect that your child has one of the specific behavioural disorders described in this book (see pages 74–107), you can discuss it first with your child's teacher, school nurse or health visitor. You can ask your GP or school doctor to refer your child to a child mental health team, which may be hospital or community based. Psychologists, psychiatrists, psychiatric nurses, mental health workers and therapists from different backgrounds with a range of specialist expertise often work closely together in a team. They will refer you to the team member who has the skill that best fits in with your needs.

Children with special needs

If your child has special needs relating, for example, to a disability caused by a physical, learning, communication, emotional or behavioural disorder, he will need help from a team of professionals as well as his parents. Different agencies may need to be involved, for example, Social Services to help you claim disability allowance, and voluntary agencies specialising in your child's condition, health and education.

Local education authority assistance

As a parent, you may need to be proactive not only in parenting your child positively, as described earlier in this book, but also in encouraging the support agencies to give you the help you need. Once your child's needs are recognised, your local educational authority (LEA) has a statutory obligation to meet your child's basic needs if he is in a comprehensive school. (This is not the case if your child is in an independent school.)

The LEA have a role in helping you assess your child's educational needs and producing an action plan for these to be met. As a parent, you have the right to ask for an assessment by an educational psychologist, to have the individual educational plan explained to you, to contribute to future plans for your child and to appeal against decisions with which you disagree.

For children with more severe problems, this can progress to a full statement of special needs, which should include in it all the recommendations of all the specialists who have been involved with your child.

Parents can request a statement if they feel that their child's special needs are not being meet, but most children's special needs can be met without this, especially as we are all getting better at identifying and helping these children.

The positive attitude of the support team available will often make enough of a difference, even if resources in terms of extra teaching, specialist input or need for computers or other equipment are inadequate Your views of what is adequate may differ from the views of your LEA. Schools are obliged to provide support so that your child can access the curriculum. They usually do not have sufficient funds to maximise your child's potential, which is what you will want, and it is important for this difference not to get in the way of working together for your child.

Support agencies and charities

Support agencies and charities specific to your child's condition can be helpful (see below and 'Useful information', page 165) in recommending what basic minimum care you can expect to get, and which educational establishments can provide this, as well as advising you about the best way to get more help.

Social problems

If you think that your main problem is a lack of support (whether it is financial, child care, housing problems, domestic violence or custodial disputes over your child's care), you are most likely to get effective help from Social Services. Social Services have a statutory role to protect children from all forms of abuse, and play a crucial role in preventing the breakdown of a home situation. They have access to services and care that other services don't. You can get the telephone number for your local service from the yellow pages.

If you are concerned that you may seriously harm your child, your child is out of control and you can no longer cope or you have a domestic crisis, Social Services will be your best port of call. Many parents don't ask for help until it is too late, fearing that their children will be taken into care against their will. This is not the aim of Social Services. If you are the one asking for the help, their job is to help you out, not criticise. Social Services are there to help you meet your child's needs. If you are on your own with no support, they can be a lifeline, providing you with local support and information about childcare, local voluntary agencies, housing, benefits, adult education and so on.

You won't get help unless you ask for it. Asking is a sign of strength, not failure.

Offending behaviour and substance abuse

The Government has recently set up youth offending teams, usually run by the council, to which you can self-refer. Specialist drug teams are also available, but you will have to make enquiries in your area as to how these can be accessed.

Sources of support
Family and community

These include relatives, friends, neighbours, other parents from your child's school or playgroup, religious leaders and recommended child carers. Local teenagers can be recruited from your local high school or via personal contacts to provide babysitting, or support during 'rush hour' at home, as 'tea-time' girls. They will be keen to earn extra cash at a price that you can afford, and this can also free you up to create some time out for you. Look at the notices in community and sports centres for activities you may wish to take up in your time out. Leisure centres may have inexpensive exercise, relaxation, yoga, meditation, or other enjoyable or interesting classes.

Information resources

Look in your local library or on the internet if you have access. There are excellent publications and websites, many of which are listed in 'Useful information', page 165. Your local yellow pages may have a helpful selection of community resource numbers. For example, they will list local nurseries, schools, adult educational and recreational facilities, agencies that provide childcare – nanny, childminder or au pair agencies in your area. Numbers for your local health centres and Social Services will also be in here. There are excellent telephone advice and helplines listed in 'Useful information', page 165. Many areas produce a local special needs magazine of help available in your area.

Adult education

There are many courses available from your local college of adult education, ranging from assertiveness to Zen Buddhism. Courses on parenting, child care, teaching special needs, and relaxation or alternative medicine may be helpful. You can call your local college, polytechnic, university or the Open University to find out what is available. The library and internet may also be helpful sources for courses.

Businesses

Your local health food shop, newsagents and pharmacies may have notices in their windows about local resources in your community. Your employers may offer support for their staff if you are working. Ask about occupational health at work.

Parent support groups

These may be available in your area, and you may find information about these at your child's school, local library, local newspaper, health visitor, from Social Services or from networks supporting parents with children with a particular condition. Parenting groups can be extremely valuable whatever the cause of your child's behavioural problems.

Educational authority

This is usually based in your local town hall and should have resource centres for children with special needs. Educational welfare officers attached to the schools may be able to help with school-related problems, as can educational psychologists, although getting access to one can be difficult. Your child's teacher will always be your first port of call, and every school will have a school nurse and SENCO who may be helpful if you have concerns about your child. Parent advisers are often available to help you navigate your way through the educational system in the town hall.

Private tutoring

As a result of the gap between what the LEA can afford and what you want for your child, you may find that private tutoring is helpful to meet your child's needs, if you can afford it. Ideally this is best done in coordination with the school so that work is not duplicated. Teachers in school sometimes do private tutoring, and it is usually easiest to coordinate work with the school if the private tutor also works there. Alternatively, university or high school students looking for extra money may be helpful, but people trained in special educational needs may be necessary if ordinary tutoring is not helpful. Ideally, the special needs trained person would be from your child's school but, if not, you could try to contact your local adult education college and ask for the person who teaches special needs to recommend a local tutor, or one of his or her students for work experience (this may be cheaper).

Social services

These include welfare offices, job centres, parent and

family centres, and local childminders (social services have a register). You should be able to get financial advice, as well as domestic support, in times of trouble.

Voluntary agencies

Various agencies can provide a variety of support. These include local charities (such as the Catholic Children's Society and other religious charities and Barnardos), parent support groups, adoption agencies, and women's centres and refuges. The NSPCC provides support for children exposed to cruelty of any kind. There are many voluntary agencies set up to support particular conditions. There is a list of useful addresses in 'Useful information', page 165. You will have to enquire locally to find out what is available in your area, as this can be variable.

Health service

The GP is usually the first port of call but you may be able to access nurses and health visitors directly, depending on your local practice. Local health visitors and community nurses can be a mine of information. Health visitors are very experienced at dealing with babies and pre-school children and with postnatal depression. Your GP can support you directly or can refer you or your child to a counsellor, clinical psychologist or psychiatrist, or mental health team depending on the nature of the problem. The psychiatrist can refer you on to more specialist psychotherapy services if necessary.

Private health

Some areas in the country have little resource for child mental health, and the resource for adult mental health is also variable. This varies greatly across the country with London and the south generally having better resources than the north. If there is no local resource, a very long waiting list or you are not happy with what is offered by your local NHS service, you can enquire where your closest private hospital is, and ask if they offer child mental health services. Some centres specialise in particular conditions such as specialist residential establishments for anorexia in London, and a specialist dyspraxia assessment centre in Newport (see page 172).

If there are no local private hospitals, BUPA and PPP have lists of registered child psychiatrists, and you can ask to be referred to a local person through them.

Private psychologists can also be accessed for assessment and sometimes clinical work, and dyslexia centres may be able to provide this.

You may not need to be insured to be seen privately, as long as you can pay for the treatment. Prices will vary according to need and specialist seen.

Alternative medicine

Holistic and various other therapies and other approaches may be helpful for some people, but have not been evaluated scientifically. For example, some people claim that aromatherapy can be helpful in attention deficit hyperactivity disorder (ADHD), and that acupuncture can be helpful to treat adult depression, but there are no studies to substantiate these claims. There are also reports that Chinese herbs can cause liver and kidney failure, so some of these treatments are not always without risk. There are many unsubstantiated claims for miracle cures that you must be wary of, especially for conditions in which there is no known cure. Part with your money cautiously.

If you do decide to try an alternative treatment, tell your GP what you plan to do and keep both practitioners aware of any medicines that you or your child is taking. You will have to assess whether the help offered is making a difference. You would be best advised to see a registered practitioner with a good reputation, and preferably one for whom you have a personal recommendation. You can also ask to see the person's qualifications and ask to talk to previous clients.

The National Service Framework (NSF) for Children and Young People

This recently published NSF document is a framework for providing better joined-up care for children across all agencies. This will eventually lead to better and more equitable services across the country. You can visit the website (start from www.dh.gov.uk or search through Google) for an explanation of how the system will work.

KEY POINTS

- If you can't resolve your child's behavioural problems yourself or you are feeling depressed, seek help

- Help is available through many sources, including your child's school, your GP, Social Services, support groups, and family and friends

- Check out the internet sites, books and other resources in 'Useful information' (see page 165) for more information, but be aware that not all the information on the internet is trustworthy. There is much more knowledge available to the public than ever before, and excellent sources of advice and information

- Asking for help is a resourceful activity, not a weakness. Don't wait

Conclusions

Every child is special and has endless untapped potential. Nurturing and helping children develop is one of the most rewarding tasks in life. Parents and teachers can really make a difference to children's lives, every day. Most behaviours have a reason or can be understood, and support is always available. If we understand and support our children, identifying any problems early, we can help them live a healthy and happy life.

I wish you happiness and success in enjoying your children and helping them become the best that they can be.

Useful information

We have included the following organisations because, on preliminary investigation, they may be of use to the reader. However, we do not have first-hand experience of each organisation and so cannot guarantee the organisation's integrity. The reader must therefore exercise his or her own discretion and judgement when making further enquiries.

Benefits Enquiry Line
Tel: 0800 882200
Minicom: 0800 243355
Website: www.dwp.gov.uk
N. Ireland: 0800 220674

Government agency giving information and advice on sickness and disability benefits for people with disabilities and their carers.

For parents with babies and young children
Association for Post-Natal Illness
145 Dawes Road, Fulham

London SW6 7EB
Tel: 020 7386 0868 (Mon–Fri 10am–2pm)
Website: www.apni.org

Information leaflets and support to health professionals
and anyone involved with postnatal depression. Can refer
to mothers who have recovered from postnatal depression.

Cry-sis Helpline and Support Group
BM Cry-sis
London WC1N 3XX
Helpline: 0845 122 8669
Website: www.cry-sis.org.uk

Contact this organisation if you think your baby cries
excessively. Cry-sis provides local support groups,
newsletters and publications. Please include an SAE if
you are writing.

Home-Start
2 Salisbury Road
Leicester LE1 7QR
Tel: 0116 233 9955
Helpline: 0800 068 6368
Website: www.home-start.org.uk

Offers information leaflets and parent-to-parent
support in your own home in the UK and to British
Forces overseas. Provides training to volunteers.

Meet A Mum Association (MAMA)
54 Lillington Road
Radstock BA3 3NR
Depression Alliance Perinatal Line: 0845 120 3746

(Mon–Fri 7–10pm)
Website: www.mama.co.uk

Local social gatherings and mum-to-mum contact for
mums who are depressed postnatally or feel exhausted
and isolated after the birth.

National Childbirth Trust
Alexandra House, Oldham Terrace, Acton
London W3 6NH
Breast-feeding helpline: 0870 444 8708 (8am–10pm)
Pregnancy and birth helpline: 0870 444 8709
Website: www.nctpregnancyandbabycare.com

Provides antenatal and postnatal support, information
on childbirth and parenting and useful leaflets. Pre-
and postnatal classes and breast-feeding counselling by
trained teachers.

**National Childminding Association of England
and Wales**
Royal Court, 81 Tweedy Road
Bromley, Kent BR1 1TG
Tel: 0845 880 0044
Website: www.ncma.org.uk

Promotes registered childminding in England and
Wales and provides training.

Pre-school Learning Alliance
The Fitzpatrick Building, 188 York Way
London N7 9AD
Tel: 020 7697 2500
Website: www.pre-school.org.uk

Advice, support, training publications, magazine and insurance scheme. Links 16,000 community-based pre-schools.

For single parents
One Parent Families/Gingerbread
255 Kentish Town Road
London NW5 2LX
Tel: 020 7428 5400 (Mon–Fri 9am–5pm)
Lone parent helpline: 0800 018 5026 (weekdays 9am–5pm; Wed until 8pm)
Website: www.oneparentfamilies.org.uk

National network of self-help groups for single parents and children. Free information leaflets and booklets, advice on benefits and rights, childcare and holidays. Can refer to other organisations that may be able to help.

Divorce and separation
Relate
Premier House, Caroline Court
Lakeside, Doncaster DN4 5RA
Central office tel: 0845 456 1310
Website: www.relate.org.uk

This is a relationship guidance service that helps couples with difficulties and provides confidential counselling. Also offers support to children whose parents are splitting up. Relate publications on health, sexual, self-esteem, depression, bereavement and re-marriage issues available from bookshops, libraries or via website.

Bedwetting and soiling
ERIC (Education and Resources for Improving Childhood Continence)
34 Old School House, Britannia Road, Kingswood
Bristol BS15 8DB
Helpline: 0845 370 8008 (Mon–Fri 10am–4pm)
Website: www.eric.org.uk

Offers information leaflets and advice about enuresis
and encopresis; sells bedwetting protection and alarms,
and also resource materials for professionals.

For parents of children with special needs
Council for Disabled Children
National Children's Bureau, 8 Wakley Street
London EC1V 7QE
Tel: 020 7843 1900
Website: www.ncb.org.uk/cdc

Provides a national forum for the discussion,
development and dissemination of a wide range of
policy and practice issues, relating to service provision
and support for children and young people with
disabilities and special educational needs. Publications
list of useful information leaflets sent on request.
Refers enquiries to Contact a Family.

Contact a Family
209–211 City Road
London EC1V 1JN
Tel: 020 7608 8700
Helpline: 0808 808 3555 (Mon–Fri 10am–4pm, Mon
5.30–7.30pm)

Textphone: 0808 808 3556
Website: www.cafamily.org.uk

Offers help and advice for parents of children with any special needs or disability. Can put people in similar situations in touch with local branches around the UK.

Special educational needs
Advisory Centre for Education
1C Aberdeen Studios, 22 Highbury Grove
London N5 2DQ
Tel: 020 7704 3370
Helpline: 0808 800 5793 (Mon–Fri 10am–5pm)
Order line: 020 7704 9822 for Exclusion Pack
Website: www.ace-ed.org.uk

Independent national advice centre for parents of children in state schools. Offers information and advice on the law and school issues. Also offers training.

ADHD
ADDISS Attention Deficit Information Services
PO Box 340, Edgware
Middlesex HA8 9HL
Tel: 020 8952 2800
Website: www.addiss.co.uk

Provides information, support and training. Can refer to local groups in the UK. Mail order catalogue for publications sent on request.

Asperger's syndrome
Asperger's Syndrome Foundation
The Kensington Charity Centre, 4th Floor
Charles House, 375 Kensington High Street
London W14 8QH
Website: www.aspergerfoundation.org.uk

Provides bi-monthly training seminars for parents and professionals helping those with Asperger's syndrome. Please write or email for information.

Autism
National Autistic Society
393 City Road
London EC1V 1NG
Tel: 020 7833 2299
Helpline: 0845 070 4004 (Mon–Fri 10am–4pm)
Website: www.nas.org.uk

Can give you valuable information, help and support, and put you in touch with local families who have children with similar conditions.

Dyslexia
British Dyslexia Association
Unit 8, Bracknell Beeches, Old Bracknell Lane
Bracknell RG12 7BW
Helpline: 0845 251 9002
Website: www.bdadyslexia.org.uk

Raises awareness of dyslexia; provides advice, local contact and resources.

Dyslexia Action
Park House, Wick Road
Egham, Surrey TW20 0HH
Tel: 01784 222300
Website: www.dyslexia-action.org.uk

Provides information, assessment and teaching of people with dyslexia and the training of teachers.

Dyspraxia
Dyscovery Centre
Allt-yr-yn Campus, University of Wales
Newport NP20 5DA
Tel: 01633 432330
Website: www.dyscovery.co.uk

Private assessment centre for neurodevelopmental problems, providing information and training for children and adults with living and learning difficulties.

Dyspraxia Foundation
8 West Alley, Hitchin
Herts SG5 1EG
Tel: 01462 455016
Helpline: 01462 454986 (Mon–Fri 10am–1pm)
Website: www.dyspraxiafoundation.org.uk

Offers information and support via UK network to parents and professionals. Arranges conferences for parents, carers and professionals.

For young people
YoungMinds
48–50 St John Street
London EC1M 4DG
Tel: 020 7336 8445
Parents' information service: 0800 018 2138
Website: www.youngminds.org.uk

Information and advice for parents about mental illness
in young people. Produces a leaflet called *What is
ADHD?*.

Childline
45 Folgate Street
London EC1 6GL
and
Freepost NATN 1111
London E1 6BR
Tel: 020 7650 3200
Helpline: 0800 1111 (24 hours a day)
Textphone: 0800 400222
For children living away from home, or who have been
in hospital for a long time: 0800 884444 (Mon–Fri
3.30–9.30pm; Sat, Sun 2–8pm)

Provides a free and confidential service for children and
young people in trouble or danger 24 hours a day,
every day. Comforts, advises and protects and, where a
child is in danger, works with other helping agencies to
ensure the child's protection.

Careline
Cardinal Heenan Centre, 326 High Road
Ilford, Essex IG1 1QP
Tel: 020 8514 5444
Helpline: 0845 122 8622 (Mon–Fri 10am–1pm,
7–10pm)
Website: www.carelineuk.org

Provides confidential crisis telephone counselling for
children, young people and adults on many issues,
including family, marital and relationship problems.

The Samaritans
PO Box 9090
Stirling FK8 2SA
24-hour helpline: 0845 790 9090
Minicom: 0845 790 9192
Website: www.samaritans.org

Provides confidential telephone support to people who
feel suicidal or despairing and need someone to talk
to. Local branches listed in telephone directory; most
also see visitors at certain times of the day.

Youth Access
1–2 Taylor's Yard, 67 Alderbrook Road
London SW12 8BD
Tel: 020 8772 9900
Website: www.youthaccess.org.uk

Information and referral advice about support services
throughout the UK for young people aged between 11
and 25 years.

After trauma
Cruse Bereavement Care
Cruse House, 126 Sheen Road
Richmond, Surrey TW9 1UR
Tel: 020 8939 9530
Helpline: 0844 477 9400
Young person's freephone: 0808 808 1677
Website: www.crusebereavementcare.org.uk

Look up your local address in the telephone directory.
Offers information and practical advice, sells literature
and has local branches that can provide one-to-one
counselling to people who have been bereaved.
Training in bereavement counselling for professionals.

Cruse Bereavement Care Scotland
Riverview House, Friarton Road
Perth PH2 8DP
Tel: 01738 444178
Website: www.crusescotland.org.uk

National charity offering support and counselling to
anyone, of any age, who has been bereaved by the
death of someone close.

Royal College of Psychiatrists
17 Belgrave Square
London SW1X 8PG
Tel: 020 7235 2351
Website: www.rcpsych.ac.uk/info/young.htm

Produces a series of factsheets entitled *Mental Health
and Growing Up* covering all aspects of child and adult
mental health problems and advice for parents, with

contact numbers and helpful further references. A list is available, on receipt of an SAE, from the above address. Alternatively, factsheets are also available on the college website. The Child and Adolescent Faculty at the Royal College of Psychiatrists have produced a list of useful publications, which is also available on the website.

For all parents
Children are Unbeatable! Alliance
94 White Lion Street
London N1 9PF
Tel: 020 7713 0569
Website: www.childrenareunbeatable.org.uk

An alliance of organisations seeking legal reform to give children the same protection under the law on assault as adults, and promoting positive, non-violent discipline; provides leaflets on alternatives to smacking.

Clinical Knowledge Summaries
Sowerby Centre for Health Informatics at Newcastle (SCHIN Ltd), Bede House, All Saints Business Centre
Newcastle upon Tyne NE1 2ES
Tel: 0191 243 6100
Website: www.cks.library.nhs.uk

A website mainly for GPs giving information for patients listed by disease plus named self-help organisations.

Family Welfare Association
501–505 Kingsland Road
London E8 4AU

Tel: 020 7254 6251
Website: www.fwa.org.uk

Provides direct services for people with mental health problems and children and families. Provides family and relationship support in primary care practices. Some welfare and education grants for children with special needs. Professional referral essential.

Mental Health Foundation
9th Floor, Sea Containers House, 20 Upper Ground
London SE1 9QB
Tel: 020 7803 1101
Websites: www.mentalhealth.org.uk and
www.learningdisabilities.org.uk

Offers information and help for children and adults to survive, recover from and prevent mental health problems. Undertakes research, influences policy and designs training courses for health professionals, sufferers and carers. Produces a good leaflet called *All about ADHD*.

National Institute for Health and Clinical Excellence (NICE)
MidCity Place, 71 High Holborn
London WC1V 6NA
Tel: 0845 003 7780
Website: www.nice.org.uk

Provides national guidance on the promotion of good health and the prevention and treatment of ill health. Patient information leaflets are available for each piece of guidance issued.

NSPCC (National Society for the Prevention of Cruelty to Children)
Weston House, 42 Curtain Road
London EC2A 3NH
Tel: 020 7825 2500 (admin)
Tel: 020 7825 2775 (information)
Child protection helpline (helpful for adults):
0808 800 5000
Childline: 0800 1111
Textphone: 0800 056 0566
Website: www.nspcc.org.uk

Provides information (also in Welsh and five Asian languages), advice and counselling to anyone concerned about a child's safety. Carries out research and campaigns on behalf of children. Liaises with other agencies and offers training courses for parents and professionals through 180 community-based projects in England, Wales and Northern Ireland.

The Open University
PO Box 197
Milton Keynes MK7 6BJ
Tel: 0845 300 6090 (Mon–Fri 8am–8pm, Sat 9am–5pm)
Website: www.open.ac.uk

The Faculty of Health and Social Care produces home study packs and videos on babies, children, teenagers and being a parent, which you can use individually or in groups.

Parentline Plus
520 Highgate Studios, 53–79 Highgate Road
Kentish Town, London NW5 1TL
Tel: 020 7284 5500
Helpline: 0808 800 2222
Textphone: 0800 783 6783
Website: www.parentlineplus.org.uk

For parents under stress nationally. Provides general
confidential information and runs parenting courses.
Accepts referrals via Social Services.

WellChild
16 Royal Crescent
Cheltenham, Glos GL50 3DA
Tel: 0845 458 8171
Helpline: 0808 801 0330
Website: www.wellchild.org.uk

Fundraises to support research. Trains volunteers to
help in the home.

Websites and resource information
ADHD, specific learning difficulties, dyspraxia
www.chadd.org
www.dyscovery.co.uk
www.add.org
www.additudemag.com
www.sarisolden.com
www.add.about.com
www.addconsults.com
www.geocities.com/janice13/ADD2.html
www.adhdnews.com
www.addvance.com

www.adders.org
www.addinschool.com (for teachers)

Autism/Asperger's syndrome
www.aspergersyndrome.com
www.mugsy.org
www.tonyattwood.com.au
www.aspergerfoundation.org.uk (newest
website)

Learning disabilities
www.learningdisabilities.org.uk
Electronic bulletin for children with disabilities/special
educational needs.

National Inclusive Play Network
Join this by sending an email to nipnetwork-
subscribe@yahoogroups.com (very positive outcomes –
provide information and training).

General information
www.practicalparent.org.uk

Books and further information
Learning disabilities
Cowan A. *First Impressions. Emotional and practical
support for families of a young child with a learning
disability.* Free from 020 7803 1100

Parenting
Lindenfield G. *Success from Setbacks* and other books:
*Assert Yourself, Confident Children, Emotional
Confidence, Managing Anger, The Positive Woman,*

Self Esteem, Self motivation, Super Confidence. Thorsons, 1999.

Gray J. *Men are from Mars and Women are from Venus*. Harper Collins, 2002.

Covey SR. *The Seven Habits of Highly Effective Families*. Simon & Schuster UK Ltd, 1997.

Faber A, Mazlish E. *How to talk so kids will listen and listen so kids will talk*. Piccadilly, 2001.

Forehand R, Nicholas Long N. *Parenting the Strong-Willed Child*. Contemporary Books, 2002.

Gottman J. *The Heart of Parenting. How to raise an emotionally intelligent child*. Bloomsbury, 1997.

Green C. *Toddler Taming*. London: Random Century, 1991.

Pearce J. *Tantrums and Tempers*. Thorsons, 1989.

Phillips A. *Saying 'no'*. Faber & Faber Ltd, 1999.

Hartley-Brewer E. *Positive Parenting*. London: Vermilion, 1994.

Separation and divorce
Wells R. *Helping Children Cope with Divorce*. Sheldon Press, 1989.

Focus on Families. Divorce and its effects on children. The Children's Society, 1983.

Keeping in Touch: How to help your child after separation and divorce. Booklet for parents, available from

YoungMinds Parent Info. Service: 0800 018 2138.

Sleeping problems
Douglas J, Richman N. *My Child Won't Sleep*. Harmondsworth: Penguin, 1984.

Ferber R. *Solve Your Child's Sleep Problems*. London: Dorling Kindersley, 1986.

School-related problems
Berg I, Nursten J (eds). *Unwillingly to School*. London: Gaskell, 1996.

Melville J, Subotsky F. *Does My Child Need Help? A guide for worried parents*. Optima, 1992.

Special educational needs
Special Educational Needs: A guide for parents. DFE publications. Tel: 0845 602 2260.

ADHD
Green C, Chee K. *Understanding ADD. A parent's guide to DD in children*. London: Vermilion Press, 1995

Kewley GD. *ADHD: Recognition, reality and resolution*. David Fulton, 2001.

Pentecost D. *Parenting the ADD Child*. London: Jessica Kingsley, 2000.

Taylor E. *The Hyperactive Child: A parent guide*, 2nd edn. London: Optima, 1994.

Train A. *Children Behaving Badly. Could my child have a disorder?* Souvenir Press Ltd, 2000.

Depression
Graham P, Hughes C. *So Young, So Sad, So Listen*. London: Gaskell, 1995.

Young people
Burningham S. *Young People Under Stress: A parent's guide*. London: Virago, 1994.

The internet as a source of further information
After reading this book, you may feel that you would like further information on the subject. The internet is of course an excellent place to look and there are many websites with useful information about medical disorders, related charities and support groups.

It should always be remembered, however, that the internet is unregulated and anyone is free to set up a website and add information to it. Many websites offer impartial advice and information that has been compiled and checked by qualified medical professionals. Some, on the other hand, are run by commercial organisations with the purpose of promoting their own products. Others still are run by pressure groups, some of which will provide carefully assessed and accurate information whereas others may be suggesting medications or treatments that are not supported by the medical and scientific community.

Unless you know the address of the website you want to visit – for example, www.familydoctor.co.uk – you may find the following guidelines useful when searching the internet for information.

Search engines and other searchable sites

Google (www.google.co.uk) is the most popular search engine used in the UK, followed by Yahoo! (http://uk.yahoo.com) and MSN (www.msn.co.uk). Also popular are the search engines provided by Internet Service Providers such as Tiscali and other sites such as the BBC site (www.bbc.co.uk).

In addition to the search engines that index the whole web, there are also medical sites with search facilities, which act almost like mini-search engines, but cover only medical topics or even a particular area of medicine. Again, it is wise to look at who is responsible for compiling the information offered to ensure that it is impartial and medically accurate. The NHS Direct site (www. nhsdirect.nhs.uk) is an example of a searchable medical site.

Links to many British medical charities can be found at the Association of Medical Charities' website (www.amrc.org.uk) and at Charity Choice (www.charitychoice.co.uk).

Search phrases

Be specific when entering a search phrase. Searching for information on 'cancer' will return results for many different types of cancer as well as on cancer in general. You may even find sites offering astrological information. More useful results will be returned by using search phrases such as 'lung cancer' and 'treatments for lung cancer'. Both Google and Yahoo! offer an advanced search option that includes the ability to search for the exact phrase; enclosing the search phrase in quotes, that is, 'treatments for lung cancer', will have the same effect. Limiting a search to an exact phrase reduces the number of results returned but it is best to refine a search to an exact match only if you are not getting useful results with a normal search. Adding 'UK' to your search term will bring up mainly British sites, so a good phrase might be 'lung cancer' UK (don't include UK within the quotes).

Always remember the internet is international and unregulated. It holds a wealth of valuable information but individual sites may be biased, out of date or just plain wrong. Family Doctor Publications accepts no responsibility for the content of links published in this series.

Index

Your pages

We have included the following pages because they may help you manage your illness or condition and its treatment.

Before an appointment with a health professional, it can be useful to write down a short list of questions of things that you do not understand, so that you can make sure that you do not forget anything.

Some of the sections may not be relevant to your circumstances.

We are always pleased to receive constructive criticism or suggestions about how to improve the books. You can contact us at:

Email: familydoctor@btinternet.com
Letter: Family Doctor Publications
            PO Box 4664
            Poole
            BH15 1NN

Thank you

Health-care contact details

Name:

Job title:

Place of work:

Tel:

Name:

Job title:

Place of work:

Tel:

Name:

Job title:

Place of work:

Tel:

Name:

Job title:

Place of work:

Tel:

Significant past health events – illnesses/operations/investigations/treatments

Event	Month	Year	Age (at time)

Appointments for health care

Name:

Place:

Date:

Time:

Tel:

Name:

Place:

Date:

Time:

Tel:

Name:

Place:

Date:

Time:

Tel:

Name:

Place:

Date:

Time:

Tel:

Appointments for health care

Name:

Place:

Date:

Time:

Tel:

Name:

Place:

Date:

Time:

Tel:

Name:

Place:

Date:

Time:

Tel:

Name:

Place:

Date:

Time:

Tel:

Current medication(s) prescribed by your doctor

Medicine name:

Purpose:

Frequency & dose:

Start date:

End date:

Medicine name:

Purpose:

Frequency & dose:

Start date:

End date:

Medicine name:

Purpose:

Frequency & dose:

Start date:

End date:

Medicine name:

Purpose:

Frequency & dose:

Start date:

End date:

Other medicines/supplements you are taking, not prescribed by your doctor

Medicine/treatment:

Purpose:

Frequency & dose:

Start date:

End date:

Medicine/treatment:

Purpose:

Frequency & dose:

Start date:

End date:

Medicine/treatment:

Purpose:

Frequency & dose:

Start date:

End date:

Medicine/treatment:

Purpose:

Frequency & dose:

Start date:

End date:

Questions to ask at appointments
(Note: do bear in mind that doctors work under great time pressure, so long lists may not be helpful for either of you)

Questions to ask at appointments
(Note: do bear in mind that doctors work under great time
pressure, so long lists may not be helpful for either of you)

Notes